4.00

The WIT and WISDOM of
JANE AUSTEN

The WIT and WISDOM of
JANE AUSTEN

edited by *Michael Kerrigan*

FOURTH ESTATE • LONDON

*F*irst published in Great Britain in 1996 by
Fourth Estate Limited, 6 Salem Road, London,
W2 4BU

2 4 6 8 10 9 7 5 3

A catalogue record for this book is available from the
British Library.

ISBN 1–85702–601–2

Typeset by Avon Dataset Ltd, Bidford on Avon B50 4JH
Printed and bound in Great Britain by Clays Ltd,
St. Ives plc

Contents

Introduction

Few great writers can have cut so unglamorous a figure in the world as Jane Austen did. Though her novels from the first proved popular with the reading public, among the Hampshire gentry with whom she lived and visited her abilities went unguessed at. As for her family, while treasuring her merry, irreverent conversation, they found other accomplishments more immediately praiseworthy. According to her nephew, J. Edward Austen-Leigh, who wrote a *Memoir* of his aunt in 1870, in his own old age, 'Her needlework both plain and ornamental was excellent, and might almost have put a sewing machine to shame. She was considered especially great in satin stitch.' Her younger relations, not surprisingly, were more alive to her sense of fun – 'Her performance with cup and ball was marvellous', records her nephew fondly – but they were no more able than their parents to imagine the miraculous talent that was coming to fruition in their midst as, working steadily away in the crowded parlour in the little family house at Chawton, between convivial family mealtimes, noisy games of 'Spilikens' and quiet sessions of reading and sewing, their aunt created the novels which would in time admit her to the company of England's most revered writers – and as the most enduringly readable, lovable genius of them all. Even many decades after her death, when the fame of Jane Austen extended across the world, her Hampshire neighbours were the last to know. 'A few years ago,' recalls Austen-Leigh, 'a gentleman visiting Winchester Cathedral desired to be shown Miss Austen's grave. The verger, as he pointed it out, asked, "Pray, sir, can you tell me whether there was anything particular about that lady; so many people want to know where she was buried?" '

As the sixth of seven children, Jane Austen was introduced early to the idea of her own insignificance. The Reverend George Austen had been given the neighbouring Hampshire parishes of Deane and Steventon to administer in 1764, the same year that he married Cassandra Leigh. The couple lived in Deane for the first few years, however, and it was not until 1771 that they moved, with their growing family, to the rectory at Steventon in which, in 1775, Jane would be born. By that time, her eldest brother, James, was over ten years old: he must have seemed like another adult to the young girl, kind but a little imposing; a cultivated young man of wide literary and intellectual interests, he did much to foster her early interest in books. Affable and lively as he was by temperament, her next-eldest brother, Edward, was a remote figure in a different way. By an arrangement of a sort not uncommon at the time, he had been adopted by a relation, Mr Knight, in order to relieve some of the Austen family's financial pressures. Living with his adoptive father in comparative splendour, he would eventually inherit both his name and estate; he became close to Jane in adulthood, his daughter, Fanny, becoming perhaps her favourite niece. The nearest to an underachiever the family was to produce, Henry was nonetheless a witty and likeable young man: it was his lack of steadiness, rather than any shortage of ability, which prevented his making more of a mark in a career as clergyman to which he was characteristically slow in settling. Though three years older than Jane, Cassandra, the novelist's only sister, was also to prove her lifelong friend and confidante – and the recipient of many of her most acerbic and entertaining letters. The two brothers closest to Jane in age would both rise successfully in the Navy: both Francis and Charles would attain the rank of admiral, the former finally being appointed Senior Admiral of the Fleet.

Yet if the presence of so many strong personalities taught Jane to know her place, it also guaranteed an unending flow of jokes and games. Overflowing as it was with bright, boisterous children, the rectory at Steventon was a house of hilarity: there was always an eager cast of actors for any dressing-up game or dramatic presentation, an affectionate, appreciative audience for any doggerel rhyme or skit. It was in just such a spirit of family fun that Jane Austen produced her first work of fiction: by the age of twelve she was already writing little stories and plays, by fourteen she had written the short novel, *Love and Freindship* [sic], and the stream of outrageously nonsensical (but impeccably crafted) squibs, spoofs and satires continued unabated throughout her teen-age years. Slight as these performances may be, they express opinions and interests which would reappear in Jane Austen's 'grown-up' writing: there's the same derisive disrespect for pretension, for example, the same unfoolable eye for hypocrisy. Most of all, however, there's the same irrepressible humour, for even in the darkest works of her adulthood – works like *Mansfield Park* and *Persuasion* – the same wit and mischief can be seen. In its own preposterous way, the Juvenilia establishes Jane Austen as, essentially, a comic writer with a serious side, rather than a serious writer who tells jokes. The voice of *Love and Freindship* is unmistakably the voice of *Pride and Prejudice* and *Emma*: the joyous games of girlhood were built upon by the maturing author, and refined beyond recognition, but they would never be entirely left behind.

Not that her life can have been uniformly cheerful. Quite what tragedies it comprised cannot be known for sure, since in a spirit of protectiveness for which posterity has not thanked her, Cassandra destroyed much of her sister's correspondence after her death in 1817. What griefs, what disappointments, what scandals she may have been concealing in the process will never now be known, though the speculation has afforded hundreds of scholars many thousands of hours of more or less harmless amusement. What we do know for certain is that the Reverend George Austen died in 1805, not long after retiring with his family to Bath. His widow and children moved first to Southampton and then, in 1809, to Chawton, to the little cottage on what was now Edward's Hampshire estate, in which Jane would live for most of her adult life, and complete the great works of her maturity. Of these, *Sense and Sensibility* was the first to appear, in 1811, followed in 1813 by *Pride and Prejudice*. Early versions of both of these novels had been written as much as fifteen years previously, but the author's own meticulous revision and re-revision over a number of years had been followed by a long spell gathering dust on a publisher's shelf. (Much the same thing happened to *Northanger Abbey* which, though bought by Crosby & Co. as early as 1803, would not finally appear until after Jane's death.) Once published, however, these early novels were well received: the 1814 publication of *Mansfield Park* was eagerly awaited, not least, it seems, by the Prince Regent, whose secretary wrote to Jane Austen with the idea that she might want to write a 'historical romance, illustrative of the history of the august House of Cobourg'. Delicately sidestepping this suggestion, she dedicated her next novel, *Emma* (1816), to His Royal Highness. It is hard to imagine that he can have felt himself in any way the loser. *Persuasion* was completed in 1815, but not published until after its author's death, in 1817, of Addison's disease, when Jane Austen's last-completed novel appeared alongside what was probably her first, *Northanger Abbey*. Another novel, *Sanditon*, had been left uncompleted at her death.

Yet much of Jane Austen's time will have been spent not as writer, but as daughter, sister and aunt, living the very ordinary, unassuming life of the Austens of Chawton. Theirs was a genteel, rather than a luxurious, lifestyle, for though George Austen had been a respectable clergyman and his sons would prosper in their chosen professions, the family was by no means rich. Their existence would not have been so very different from that described in the novels. They walked in the nearby woods and fields, visited and received neighbours, took tea and chatted, and generally endured and enjoyed the routine chores and treats of the genteel country society of the day. It was a quiet existence, perhaps, but anyone who has read Jane Austen's novels – or, for that matter, anyone who has browsed at any length in the present anthology – will hesitate before dismissing it as a 'narrow' or 'sheltered' one. There's some superficial truth in the charge, of course. Jane Austen's reader can undoubtedly feel a sense of being removed from the concerns of the wider world. It can be hard for the reader of *Sense and Sensibility* to remember that its author grew up and wrote in an age wracked by revolution and war. Yet as her reader comes quickly to realise, Jane Austen's world contains the wider one. Polite and contrived as it may at first seem, the social round of the rural gentry conceals beneath its civilised surface all the bloodiest instincts of human nature, all the raw aggression and competition of social existence. If life for Austen's heroines can at times seem like one long husband-hunt, the business (and it was indeed a business) of courtship and marriage was by no means a trivial one in an age when other professions than wifehood were not open to women. To the young girl who knew she had but one chance of happiness, the drawing room a jungle, the ball a battlefield: if marriage might involve a life sentence with a pompous bore or, worse, a drunken brute, spinsterhood could at best mean humiliating dependence and at worst destitution. Yet if Jane Austen saw through the mythology of romantic love and marriage to the squalid struggle for economic advantage which it all too often concealed, she saw too that marriage could, on occasion, represent real love, and bring men and women alike a degree of personal fulfilment that made every day a joy. A sceptic, then, but still at heart a believer, Jane Austen brought together romance and realism in her writing. No other writer, before or since, has managed to combine as thrillingly as she does the competing qualities of yearning eroticism, ardent idealism . . . and shrewd common sense.

Jane Austen did not need to go out into the world to find the world. A writer with an eye like hers for the weakness, the folly, the malice of humanity, found the world daily beating a path to her door, presenting itself in every item of gossip, in every name-dropping anecdote, in every overbearing neighbour, in every brash, boastful dinner guest and in every calculating caller. Yet, far too intelligent a writer to despair, she saw other things too. In the cheerful endurance of the sick, the patient optimism of the poor, in the everyday courage of the bereaved and abandoned – and, of course, in the occasional happy marriage! – she saw just how noble, how worthwhile human existence might be for those who were prepared to live honestly and well. These qualities are timeless – as instantly recognisable to us as they were to the family and friends who were Jane Austen's first readers nearly two centuries ago. Not only did Jane Austen's fiction encompass her world – it encompasses our world too.

Works of Jane Austen

'Jack and Alice', 'The Adventures of Mr Harley' and 'The Three Sisters', from VOLUME THE FIRST, written 1787–90.

'Love and Freindship', written 1790.

'A History of England', written 1791.

'Lesley Castle', written 1792.

'Catharine, or the Bower', written 1792–3.

LADY SUSAN, written around 1795, never submitted for publication.

SENSE and SENSIBILITY, written 1795 as 'Elinor and Marianne', renamed and revised 1797 and published 1811.

PRIDE and PREJUDICE, written 1796–7 as 'First Impressions', rejected by publisher; revised and renamed version published 1813.

THE WATSONS, begun 1804; abandoned incomplete on father's death in 1805.

MANSFIELD PARK, begun 1811, published 1814.

EMMA, written 1814–15, published 1815.

'Plan of a Novel', written 1816.

PERSUASION, written 1815–16, published posthumously 1818.

NORTHANGER ABBEY, written as 'Susan', 1797–8; revised, re-named version published posthumously 1818, together with *Persuasion*.

SANDITON, begun 1817, left uncompleted on Jane Austen's death.

Love and Friendship

What a strange thing love is!
(EMMA)

Love conquers all; young love, at least:

*W*hen any two young people take it into their heads to marry, they are pretty sure by perseverance to carry their point, be they ever so poor, or ever so imprudent, or ever so little likely to be necessary to each other's ultimate comfort.   PERSUASION

On the inevitability of young love, and the need for emotional occupation:

*H*e was, at that time, a remarkably fine young man, with a great deal of intelligence, spirit and brilliancy; and Anne an extremely pretty girl, with gentleness, modesty, taste, and feeling. Half the sum of attraction, on either side, might have been enough, for he had nothing to do, and she had hardly any body to love; but the encounter of such lavish recommendations could not fail. They were gradually acquainted, and when acquainted, rapidly and deeply in love.

PERSUASION

The violence of young love:

. . . the tyrannic influence of youth on youth . . .

EMMA

Love at first sight?:

'*W*ill you tell me how long you have loved him?'

'It has been coming on so gradually, that I hardly know when it began. But I believe I must date it from my first seeing his beautiful grounds at Pemberley.'

PRIDE AND PREJUDICE

On the duties of romantic love:
Marianne would have felt herself very inexcusable had she been able to sleep at all the first night after parting from Willoughby...

SENSE AND SENSIBILITY

On the love-prone personality:
Harriet was one of those, who, having once begun, would be always in love.

EMMA

On getting ahead of oneself:
A lady's imagination is very rapid; it jumps from admiration to love, from love to matrimony in a moment.

PRIDE AND PREJUDICE

The ideal mate . . . a mythical beast?:
I could not be happy with a man whose taste did not in every point coincide with my own. He must enter into all my feelings; the same books, the same music must charm us both . . . the more I know of the world, the more am I convinced that I shall never see a man whom I can really love. I require so much!

SENSE AND SENSIBILITY

On the kinship of loving spirits:
Any thing interests between those who love; and any

thing will serve as introduction to what is near the heart.   EMMA

Talk as the food of love:
Though a very few hours spent in the hard labour of incessant talking will dispatch more subjects than can really be in common between any two rational creatures, yet with lovers it is different. Between *them* no subject is finished, no communication is even made, till it has been made at least twenty times over.

SENSE AND SENSIBILITY

On love's sickness:
This sensation of listlessness, weariness, stupidity, this disinclination to sit down and employ myself, this feeling of every thing's being dull and insipid about the house! – I must be in love . . .   EMMA

At what moment can love be said to start?:
I cannot fix on the hour, or the spot, or the look, or the words, which laid the foundation. It is too long ago. I was in the middle before I knew I *had* begun.

PRIDE AND PREJUDICE

Love, like charity, should begin at home:
As to any real knowledge of a person's disposition that Bath, or any public place, can give – it is all nothing; there can be no knowledge. It is only by seeing women

in their own homes, among their own set, just as they always are, that you can form any just judgement. Short of that, it is all guess and luck – and will generally be ill-luck.   EMMA

On the joys of feeling just a little in love:
She was very often thinking of him, and quite impatient for a letter, that she might know how he was, how were his spirits . . . But, on the other hand, she could not admit herself to be unhappy, nor, after the first morning, to be less disposed for employment than usual; she was still busy and cheerful; and, pleasing as he was, she could yet imagine him to have faults; and farther, though thinking of him so much, and as she sat drawing or working, forming a thousand amusing schemes for the progress and close of their attachment, fancying interesting dialogues, and inventing elegant letters, the conclusion of every imaginary declaration on his side was that she *refused him*.

EMMA

Men may have to be prompted into love:
There is so much of gratitude or vanity in almost any attachment, that it is not safe to leave any to itself. We can all *begin* freely – a slight preference is natural enough; but there are very few of us who have heart enough to be really in love without encouragement. In

nine cases out of ten, a woman had better show *more* affection than she feels.   PRIDE AND PREJUDICE

A Lakeland holiday for one crossed in love:
Adieu to disappointment and spleen. What are men to rocks and mountains?   PRIDE AND PREJUDICE

On compatibility
It is not time or opportunity that is to determine intimacy; – it is disposition alone. Seven years would be insufficient to make some people acquainted with each other, and seven days are more than enough for others.
    SENSE AND SENSIBILITY

Economy of affability:
I do not want people to be very agreeable, as it saves me the trouble of liking them a great deal.
    (Letter to her sister Cassandra, 24 December 1798)

What friends are for:
Friendship is certainly the finest balm for the pangs of disappointed love.   NORTHANGER ABBEY

Qualified euphoria, as the heroine of 'Jack and Alice', written when Jane Austen was twelve, makes a new friend:
The perfect form, the beautifull face, and elegant manners of Lucy so won on the affections of Alice that

when they parted, which was not till after Supper, she assured her that except her Father, Brother, Uncles, Aunts, Cousins and other relations, Lady Williams, Charles Adams and a few dozen more of particular freinds, she loved her better than almost any other person in the world.

Faint friendship:
I respect Mrs Chamberlayne for doing her hair well, but cannot feel a more tender sentiment.

(Letter to her sister Cassandra, 12 May 1801)

Nothing pleases us like the success of our friends . . .
unless of course it's their failure:
*M*rs Allen was now quite happy – quite satisfied with Bath. She had found some acquaintance, had been so lucky too as to find in them the family of a most worthy old friend; and, as the completion of good fortune, had found these friends by no means so expensively dressed as herself.   NORTHANGER ABBEY

On the dangers of an unequal friendship:
I think her the very worst sort of companion that Emma could possibly have. She knows nothing herself, and looks upon Emma as knowing every thing. She is a flatterer in all her ways; and so much the worse, because undesigned. Her ignorance is hourly flattery.

EMMA

Sheer inertia shores up some friendships, suggests the fifteen-year-old author in 'Lesley Castle':

To tell you the truth, our freindship arose rather from Caprice on her side than Esteem on mine. We spent two or three days together with a Lady in Berkshire with whom we both happened to be connected. During our visit, the Weather being remarkably bad, and our party particularly stupid, she was so good as to conceive a violent partiality for me, which very soon settled into a downright Freindship, and ended in an established correspondence. She is probably by this time as tired of me, as I am of her; but as she is too polite and I am too civil to say so, our letters are still as frequent and affectionate as ever, and our Attachment as firm and sincere as when it first commenced.

*M*arriage

*I am no match-maker — being much too well aware of
the uncertainty of all human events and calculations.*

(PERSUASION)

On the correct response to a proposal of marriage:
What did she say? – Just what she ought, of course. A lady always does. – She said enough to show there need not be despair – and to invite him to say more himself.

EMMA

On a woman's right to choose, and refuse:
A woman is not to marry a man merely because she is asked, or because he is attached to her, and can write a tolerable letter.

EMMA

And man's inability to understand this . . .
It is always incomprehensible to a man that a woman should ever refuse an offer of marriage. A man always imagines a woman to be ready for anybody who asks her.

EMMA

The economic motive:
Single women have a dreadful propensity for being poor – which is one very strong argument in favour of Matrimony . . .

(Letter to her niece Fanny Knight, 13 March 1817)

Murphy's law of marriage:
There certainly are not so many men of large fortune in the world, as there are pretty women to deserve them.

MANSFIELD PARK

A gold-digger's advice:

I would have everybody marry if they can do it properly; I do not like to have people throw themselves away; but everybody should marry as soon as they can do it to advantage. MANSFIELD PARK

And an author's warning . . .

*N*othing can be compared to the misery of being bound *without* Love, bound to one, & preferring another.

(Letter to her niece Fanny Knight, 30 November 1814)

A perfect bride:

*T*he charming Augusta Hawkins, in addition to all the usual advantages of perfect beauty and merit, was in possession of an independent fortune, of so many thousands as would always be called ten; a point of some dignity, as well as some convenience . . . EMMA

And a possible groom?:

*H*er brother was not handsome; no, when they first saw him, he was absolutely plain . . . but still he was the gentleman, with a pleasing address. The second meeting proved him not so very plain; he was plain, to be sure, but then he had so much countenance, and his teeth were so good, and he was so well made, that one soon forgot he was plain; and after a third interview, after dining in company with him at the parsonage, he was no longer allowed to be called so by any body. He was, in fact, the most agreeable young man the sisters had ever known, and they were equally delighted with him. Miss Bertram's engagement made him in equity the property of Julia, of which Julia was fully aware, and before he had been at Mansfield a week, she was quite ready to be fallen in love with. MANSFIELD PARK

High-minded idealism versus cheerful practicality – two sisters dispute:

'To be so bent on marriage – to pursue a man merely for the sake of situation – is a sort of thing that shocks me; I cannot understand it. Poverty is a great evil, but to a woman of education and feeling it ought not, it cannot be the greatest. – I would rather be a teacher at a school (and I can think of nothing worse) than marry a man I did not like.'

'I would rather do anything than be a teacher at a school – ' said her sister. 'I have been at school, Emma, and know what a life they lead you: *you* never have. – I should not like marrying a disagreeable man any more than yourself, – but I do not think there *are* very many disagreeable men; – I think I could like any good humoured man with a comfortable income.'

THE WATSONS

Marriage à la mode:

*M*r Rushworth was from the first struck with the

beauty of Miss Bertram, and being inclined to marry, soon fancied himself in love. He was a heavy young man, with not more than common sense; but as there was nothing disagreeable in his figure or address, the young lady was well pleased with her conquest. Being now in her twenty-first year, Maria Bertram was beginning to think matrimony a duty; and as a marriage with Mr Rushworth would give her the enjoyment of a larger income than her father's, as well as ensure her the house in town, which was now a prime object, it became, by the same rule of moral obligation, her evident duty to marry Mr Rushworth if she could.

MANSFIELD PARK

And the ceremony . . .
It was a very proper wedding. The bride was elegantly dressed – the two bridesmaids were duly inferior – her father gave her away – her mother stood with salts in her hand, expecting to be agitated – her aunt tried to cry – and the service was impressively read . . .

MANSFIELD PARK

Another young bride to the (sacrificial) altar:
In as short a time as Mr Collins's long speeches would allow, every thing was settled between them to the satisfaction of both; and as they entered the house, he earnestly entreated her to name the day that was to make him the happiest of men; and though such a

solicitation must be waived for the present, the lady felt no inclination to trifle with his happiness. The stupidity with which he was favoured by nature, must guard his courtship from any charm that could make a woman wish for its continuance; and Miss Lucas, who accepted him solely from the pure and disinterested desire of an establishment, cared not how soon that establishment were gained . . . Mr Collins to be sure was neither sensible nor agreeable; his society was irksome, and his attachment to her must be imaginary. But still he would be her husband.   PRIDE AND PREJUDICE

Love above all:
*A*nything is to be preferred or endured rather than marrying without Affection.
(Letter to her niece Fanny Knight, 18 November 1814)

A young lady weighs the odds, from 'The Three Sisters',
written when Jane Austen was twelve, by which time the
future novelist had already acquired a certain scepticism
where the idea of romantic love was concerned:
*M*y dear Fanny,
I am the happiest creature in the World, for I have received an offer of marriage from Mr Watts. It is the first I have ever had and I hardly know how to value it enough . . . I do not intend to accept it, at least I believe not, but as I am not quite certain I gave him an

equivocal answer and left him . . . He is quite an old Man, about two and thirty, very plain *so* plain that I cannot bear to look at him. He is extremely disagreeable and I hate him more than any body else in the world. He has a large fortune and will make great Settlements on me; but then he is very healthy . . .

An unmemorable marriage, as recorded in one of several miniature mock-novels Jane Austen wrote as a twelve-year-old. 'The Adventures of Mr Harley', given here complete, was dedicated to her beloved elder brother Francis William Austen, then himself a midshipman in the Royal Navy.

Mr Harley was one of many Children. Destined by his father for the Church and by his Mother for the Sea, desirous of pleasing both, he prevailed on Sir John to obtain for him a Chaplaincy on board a Man of War. He accordingly, cut his Hair and sailed.

In half a year he returned and set-off in the Stage Coach for Hogsworth Green, the seat of Emma. His fellow travellers were, A man without a Hat, Another with two, An old maid and a young Wife.

This last appeared about 17 with fine dark Eyes and an elegant Shape; in short Mr Harley soon found out, that she was his Emma and recollected he had married her a few weeks before he left England.

Lines 'On the Marriage of a Middle-aged Flirt with a Mr Wake, whom it was Supposed she would Scarcely have Accepted in her Youth' (recalled by her nephew, J. Edward Austen-Leigh):

Maria, good-humoured, and handsome, and tall,
  For a husband was at her last stake;
And having in vain danced at many a ball,
  Is now happy to *jump at a Wake*.

Marriage the only meal-ticket:

Without thinking highly either of men or of matrimony, marriage had always been her object; it was the only honourable provision for well-educated young women of small fortune, and however uncertain of giving happiness, must be their pleasantest preservative from want.   PRIDE AND PREJUDICE

Money, not marriage, talks:

It is poverty only which makes celibacy contemptible to a generous public! A single woman, with a very narrow income, must be a ridiculous, disagreeable, old maid! The proper sport of boys and girls; but a single woman, of good fortune, is always respectable, and may be as sensible and pleasant as anybody else.

EMMA

Have money, will marry:
It is a truth universally acknowledged, that a single man in possession of a good fortune, must be in want of a wife.   PRIDE AND PREJUDICE

Marriage as confidence trick:
There is not one in a hundred of either sex, who is not taken in when they marry. Look where I will, I see that it *is* so; and I feel that it *must* be so, when I consider that it is, of all transactions, the one in which people expect most from others, and are least honest themselves . . . speaking from my own observation, it is a manoeuvring business. I know so many who have married in the full expectation and confidence of some one particular advantage in the connection, or accomplishment or good quality in the person, who have found themselves entirely deceived, and been obliged to put up with exactly the reverse! What is this, but a take in?

                                        MANSFIELD PARK

Lust is no substitute for love:
How little of permanent happiness could belong to a couple who were only brought together because their passions were stronger than their virtue . . .

                                        PRIDE AND PREJUDICE

On the pitfalls of an unequal marriage:

A more equal match might have greatly improved him . . . a woman of real understanding might have given more consequence to his character, and more usefulness, rationality, and elegance to his habits and pursuits . . .   PERSUASION

The lessons of matrimony:

Husbands and wives generally understand when opposition will be vain.   PERSUASION

The joys of married life: a fractious wife and her laconic husband join battle:

'You have no compassion on my poor nerves.'

'You mistake me, my dear. I have a high respect for your nerves. They are my old friends. I have heard you mention them with consideration these twenty years at least.'   PRIDE AND PREJUDICE

A husband's stoicism in marriage:

To his wife he was very little otherwise indebted than as her ignorance and folly had contributed to his amusement. This is not the sort of happiness which a man would in general wish to owe to his wife; but where other powers of entertainment are wanting, the true philosopher will derive benefit from such as are given.   PRIDE AND PREJUDICE

A qualified romanticism:

Lady Sondes' match surprises, but does not offend me; had her first marriage been of affection, or had there been a grown-up single daughter, I should not have forgiven her; but I consider everybody as having a right to marry *once* in their lives for love, if they can . . .

(Letter to her sister Cassandra, 27 December 1808)

Why shouldn't a widow remarry?:

That Lady Russell, of steady age and character, and extremely well provided for, should have no thought of a second marriage, needs no apology to the public, which is rather apt to be unreasonably discontented when a woman *does* marry again, than when she does not . . .   PERSUASION

On the need for certainty in marriage:

I lay it down as a general rule . . . that if a woman *doubts* as to whether she should accept a man or not, she certainly ought to refuse him. If she can hesitate to say 'Yes,' she ought to say 'No' directly. It is not a state to be safely entered into with doubtful feelings, with half a heart.   EMMA

On the mystery of when women fall in love:

Till it does come, you know, we women never mean

to have any body. It is a thing of course among us, that every man is refused – till he offers.

PERSUASION

On not airing one's clean linen in public:
We have heard nothing fresh from Anna. I trust she is very comfortable in her new home. Her Letters have been very sensible & satisfactory, with no *parade* of happiness, which I liked them the better for. – I have often known young married Women write in a way I did not like, in that respect.
(Letter to her niece Fanny Knight, 18 November 1814)

For better, for best . . .
Marriage is a great Improver.
(Letter to her sister Cassandra, 20 November 1808)

And finally, Jane Austen at her acerbic best – or worst:
Mrs Hall, of Sherborne, was brought to bed yesterday of a dead child, some weeks before she expected, owing to a fright. I suppose she happened unawares to look at her husband.
(Letter to her sister Cassandra, 27 October 1798)

Men and Women

What strange creatures we are!
(Letter to her niece Fanny Knight, 18 November 1814)

*One young man as seen through two different pairs of
eyes:*

'And what sort of a young man is he?'

'As good a kind of fellow as ever lived, I assure
you. A very decent shot, and there is not a bolder rider
in England.'

'And is that all you can say for him?' cried
Marianne, indignantly. 'But what are his manners on
more intimate acquaintance? What his pursuits, his
talents and genius?'

Sir John was rather puzzled.

'Upon my soul,' said he, 'I do not know much
about him as to all *that*. But he is a pleasant, good
humoured fellow, and has got the nicest little black
bitch of a pointer I ever saw. Was she out with him
today?'

But Marianne could no more satisfy him as to the
colour of Mr Willoughby's pointer, than he could
describe to her the shades of his mind.

SENSE AND SENSIBILITY

And two different languages . . . :

This is all that I can relate of the how, where, and
when. Your friend Harriet will make a much longer
history when you see her. – She will give you all the
minute particulars, which only woman's language can
make interesting. – In our communications we deal
only in the great. EMMA

Of measurement male and female:

'I am really not tired, which I almost wonder at; for we must have walked at least a mile in this wood. Do not you think we have?'

'Not half a mile,' was his sturdy answer; for he was not yet so much in love as to measure distance, or reckon time, with feminine lawlessness.

'Oh! You do not consider how much we have wound about. We have taken such a very serpentine course; and the wood itself must be half a mile long in a straight line, for we have never seen the end of it yet, since we left the first great path.'

'But if you remember, before we left that first great path, we saw directly to the end of it. We looked down the whole vista, and saw it closed by iron gates, and it could not have been more than a furlong in length.'

'Oh! I know nothing of your furlongs, but I am sure it is a very long wood; and that we have been winding in and out ever since we came into it; and therefore when I say that we have walked a mile in it, I must speak within compass.'

'We have been exactly a quarter of an hour,' said Edmund, taking out his watch. 'Do you think we are walking four miles an hour?'

'Oh! do not attack me with your watch. A watch is always too fast or too slow. I cannot be dictated to by a watch.'   MANSFIELD PARK

*On the philistinism of men, and the futility of female
vanity:*

Man only can be aware of the insensibility of man
towards a new gown. It would be mortifying to the
feelings of many ladies, could they be made to understand how little the heart of man is affected by what is
costly or new in their attire; how little it is biased by the
texture of their muslin, and how unsusceptible of
peculiar tenderness towards the spotted, the sprigged,
the mull or the jackonet. Woman is fine for her own
satisfaction alone. No man will admire her the more, no
woman will like her the better for it. Neatness and
fashion are enough for the former, and a something of
shabbiness or impropriety will be the most endearing
to the latter . . .   NORTHANGER ABBEY

On female illusions, and male exploitation:

Women fancy admiration means more than it does . . .
And men take care that they should.

PRIDE AND PREJUDICE

Division of labour:

If there is any thing disagreeable going on, men are
always sure to get out of it . . .

PERSUASION

As a lamb to the slaughter . . . :

I never saw a girl of her age bid fairer to be the sport

of mankind. Her feelings are tolerably lively, and she is so charmingly artless in their display, as to afford the most reasonable hope of her being ridiculed and despised by every man who sees her.

Artlessness will never do in love matters, and that girl is born a simpleton who has it either by nature or affectation.   LADY SUSAN

No catching the right man, no escaping the wrong:
Every young lady has at some time or other known the same agitation. All have been, or at least all have believed themselves to be, in danger from the pursuit of some one whom they wished to avoid; and all have been anxious for the attentions of some one whom they wished to please.   NORTHANGER ABBEY

On Romantic heroism:
He then departed, to make himself still more interesting, in the midst of an heavy rain.

                                          SENSE AND SENSIBILITY

On the attractions of being stupid:
A good-looking girl, with an affectionate heart and a very ignorant mind, cannot fail of attracting a clever young man . . .   NORTHANGER ABBEY

The discreet charm of the fiancée:
An engaged woman is always more agreeable than a disengaged. She is satisfied with herself. Her cares are over, and she feels that she may exert all her powers of pleasing without suspicion. All is safe with a lady engaged; no harm can be done.

MANSFIELD PARK

A romantic young lady on the duties of manhood:
That is what I like; that is what a young man ought to be. Whatever be his pursuits, his eagerness in them should know no moderation, and leave him no sense of fatigue.

SENSE AND SENSIBILITY

On the duties of manhood – two sisters compare notes:
'He is just what a young man ought to be,' said she, 'sensible, good humoured, lively; and I never saw such happy manners! – so much ease, with such perfect good breeding!'

'He is also handsome . . . which a young man ought likewise to be, if he possibly can. His character is thereby complete.'

PRIDE AND PREJUDICE

On the tantalising nature of indifference:
I never was so long in company with a girl in my life – trying to entertain her – and succeed so ill! Never

met with a girl who looked so grave on me! I must try
to get the better of this . . .'

'Foolish fellow! And so that is her attraction after
all! This it is – her not caring about you – which gives
her such a soft skin . . . and gives her all these charms
and graces!'   MANSFIELD PARK

There's no pleasing a woman:
What strange creatures we are! – It seems as if your
being secure of him (as you say yourself) had made you
Indifferent.
(Letter to her niece Fanny Knight, 18 November 1814)

*The twelve-year-old Jane Austen on male beauty, from
'The Three Sisters':*
He is rather plain to be sure, but then what is Beauty
in a Man; if he has but a genteel figure and a sensible
looking Face it is quite sufficient.

A woman cannot be too particular:
We do not often look upon fine young men, well-bred
and agreeable. We must not be nice and ask for all the
virtues into the bargain.   EMMA

On the strange appeal of a straightforward man:
Without his being a man of the world or an elder
brother, without any of the arts of flattery or the gaieties
of small talk, he began to be agreeable to her. She felt it

to be so, though she had not foreseen and could hardly understand it; for he was not pleasant by any common rule, he talked no nonsense, he paid no compliments, his opinions were unbending, his attentions tranquil and simple. There was a charm, perhaps, in his sincerity, his steadiness, his integrity . . .

MANSFIELD PARK

On flirtation as power-play:
There is exquisite pleasure in subduing an insolent spirit, in making a person pre-determined to dislike, acknowledge one's superiority. I have disconcerted him already by my calm reserve; and it shall be my endeavour to humble the pride of these self-important De Courcies still lower, to convince Mrs Vernon that her sisterly cautions have been bestowed in vain . . .

LADY SUSAN

Admiration is one thing, infidelity another:
No man is offended by another man's admiration of the woman he loves; it is the woman only who can make it a torment.

NORTHANGER ABBEY

Who loves better? A man and woman debate; him first:
I will not allow it to be more man's nature than woman's to be inconstant and forget those they do love, or have loved. I believe the reverse. I believe in a true analogy between our bodily frames and our mental; and

that as our bodies are the strongest, so are our feelings; capable of bearing most rough usage, and riding out the heaviest weather.'

'Your feelings may be the strongest,' replied Anne, 'but the same spirit of analogy will authorise me to assert that ours are the most tender. Man is more robust than woman, but he is not longer-lived; which exactly explains my view of the nature of their attachments. Nay, it would be too hard upon you, if it were otherwise. You have difficulties, and privations, and dangers enough to struggle with. You are always labouring and toiling, exposed to every risk and hardship. Your home, country, friends, all quitted. Neither time, nor health, nor life, to be called your own. It would be too hard indeed . . . if woman's feelings were to be added to all this.'

But history and literature are on his side, he says:
'I do not think I ever opened a book in my life which had not something to say upon women's inconstancy. Songs and proverbs, all talk of woman's fickleness. But perhaps you will say, these were all written by men.'

'Perhaps I shall. – Yes, yes, if you please, no reference to examples in books. Men have had every advantage of us in telling their own story. Education has been theirs in so much higher a degree; the pen has been in their hands. I will not allow books to prove any thing.'   PERSUASION

A woman's love as compared with a man's:

God forbid that I should undervalue the warm and faithful feelings of any of my fellow-creatures. I should deserve utter contempt if I dared to suppose that true attachment and constancy were known only by woman. No, I believe you capable of every thing great and good in your married lives. I believe you equal to every important exertion, and to every domestic forbearance, so long as — if I may be allowed the expression, so long as you have an object. I mean, while the woman you love lives, and lives for you. All the privilege I claim for my own sex (it is not a very enviable one, you need not covet it) is that of loving longest, when existence or when hope is gone. PERSUASION

Youth and Age

One does not care for girls till they are grown up.
(Letter to her niece Anna Austen, 9 September 1814)

On the appeal of children:

Such attractions as are by no means unusual in children of two or three years old; an imperfect articulation, an earnest desire of having his own way, many cunning tricks, and a great deal of noise . . .

SENSE AND SENSIBILITY

A doting mother watches her offspring at play:

She saw with maternal complacency all the impertinent encroachments and mischievous tricks to which her cousins submitted. She saw their sashes untied, their hair pulled about their ears, their workbags searched, and their knives and scissors stolen away, and felt no doubt of its being a reciprocal enjoyment.

SENSE AND SENSIBILITY

A model of little-girlish perfection, from 'Lesley Castle', written when Jane Austen was fifteen:

But why do I thus dwell on myself? Let me rather repeat the praise of our dear little Neice the innocent Louisa, who is at present sweetly smiling in a gentle Nap, as she reposes on the Sofa. The dear Creature is just turned of two years old; as handsome as tho' 2 and 20, as sensible as tho' 2 and 30, and as prudent as tho' 2 and 40. To convince you of this, I must inform you that she has a very fine complexion and very pretty features, that she already knows the two first Letters in the Alphabet, and that she never tears her frocks . . .

On the young people of the day:

Our little visitor has just left us, & left us highly pleased with her; – she is a nice, natural, openhearted, affectionate girl, with all the ready civility which one sees in the best Children in the present day; – so unlike anything that I was myself at her age, that I am often all astonishment & shame.

(Letter to her sister Cassandra, 8 February 1807)

A girl grows up:

She had a thin awkward figure, a sallow skin without colour, dark lank hair, and strong features; – so much for her person; – and not less unpropitious for heroism seemed her mind. She was fond of all boys' plays, and greatly preferred cricket not merely to dolls, but to the more heroic enjoyments of infancy, nursing a dormouse, feeding a canary-bird, or watering a rose-bush. Indeed she had no taste for a garden; and if she gathered flowers at all, it was chiefly for the pleasure of mischief – at least so it was conjectured from her always preferring those which she was forbidden to take . . . she was moreover noisy and wild, hated confinement and cleanliness, and loved nothing so well in the world as rolling down the green slope at the back of the house . . . At fifteen, appearances were mending; she began to curl her hair and long for balls; her complexion improved; her features were softened by plumpness and colour, her eyes gained more animation, and her figure more consequence. Her love of dirt gave way to an inclination for finery, and she grew clean as she grew smart; she had now the pleasure of sometimes hearing her father and mother remark on her personal improvement. 'Catherine grows quite a good-looking girl, – she is almost pretty to day,' were words which caught her ears now and then; and how welcome were the sounds!   NORTHANGER ABBEY

Romance, the duty of youth:
She had been forced into prudence in her youth, she learned romance as she grew older – the natural sequence of an unnatural beginning.

                                                        PERSUASION

She goes on now as young ladies of seventeen ought to do, admired and admiring . . .
    (Letter to her sister Cassandra, 24 December 1798)

The post, as seen by a world-weary old man and an
    ardent young woman:
The post-office has a great charm at one period of our lives. When you have lived to my age, you will begin to think letters are never worth going through the rain for.'

    There was a little blush . . .

    'I cannot expect that simply growing older should

make me indifferent about letters.'

'Indifferent! Oh! no – I never conceived you could become indifferent. Letters are no matter of indifference; they are generally a very positive curse.'

'You are speaking of letters of business; mine are letters of friendship.'

'I have often thought them the worst of the two,' replied he coolly. 'Business, you know, may bring money, but friendship hardly ever does.'

EMMA

On her niece's forgivable folly – fortunately, over nothing more serious than a cap and gown:

I consider it as a thing of course at her time of Life – one of the sweet taxes of youth to chuse in a hurry & make bad bargains.

(Letter to her sister Cassandra, 23 September 1813)

No fool like a young (male) fool:

*T*he notions of a young man of one or two and twenty . . . as to what is necessary in manners to make him quite the thing, are more absurd, I believe, than those of any other set of beings in the world. The folly of the means they often employ is only to be equalled by the folly of what they have in view.

PERSUASION

On the censoriousness of youth:

'A woman of seven and twenty,' said Marianne, after pausing a moment, 'can never hope to feel or inspire affection again . . .' SENSE AND SENSIBILITY

On the social pretensions of youth:

Like other young ladies she is considerably genteeler than her parents.

(Letter to her sister Cassandra, 14 September 1804)

On the effect of flattery on inexperience:

Had she been older or vainer, such attacks might have done little; but, where youth and diffidence are united, it requires uncommon steadiness of reason to resist the attraction of being called the most charming girl in the world . . . NORTHANGER ABBEY

On the resilience of youth:

To youth and natural cheerfulness . . . though under temporary gloom at night, the return of day will hardly fail to bring return of spirits. The youth and cheerfulness of morning are in happy analogy, and of powerful operation; and if the distress be not poignant enough to keep the eyes unclosed, they will be sure to open to sensation of softened pain and brighter hope.

EMMA

On the relationship between age and beauty:

It sometimes happens, that a woman is handsomer at twenty-nine than she was ten years before; and, generally speaking, if there has been neither ill health nor anxiety, it is a time at which scarcely any charm has been lost.   PERSUASION

On growing old gracefully:

The room was tolerably full, & there were perhaps thirty couple of Dancers; – the melancholy part was, to see so many dozen young Women standing by without partners . . . It was the same room in which we danced 15 years ago! – I thought it all over – & in spite of the shame of being so much older, felt with thankfulness that I was quite as happy now as then.

(Letter to her sister Cassandra, 9 December 1808)

Home and Family

Good apple pies are a considerable part of
our domestic happiness.
(Letter to her sister Cassandra, 17 October 1815)

The first rule of housekeeping:

My mother desires me to tell you that I am a very good housekeeper, which I have no reluctance in doing, because I really think it my peculiar excellence, and for this reason — I always take care to provide such things as please my own appetite, which I consider as the chief merit of housekeeping.

(Letter to her sister Cassandra, 17 November 1798)

The perfect tenant:

A lady, without a family, was the very best preserver of furniture in the world.   PERSUASION

Never mind the quality, count the limbs:

A family of ten children will be always called a fine family, where there are heads and arms and legs enough for the number.   NORTHANGER ABBEY

Some advice on family planning:

Good Mrs Deedes! — I hope she will get the better of this Marianne, & then I wd recommend to her & Mr D. the simple regimen of separate rooms.

(Letter to her niece Fanny Knight, 20 February 1817)

A father's guide to childcare:

You have your sister's letter, and every thing is down at full length there, we may be sure. My charge would be much more concise than hers, and probably not much in the same spirit; all that I have to recommend being comprised in, do not spoil them, and do not physic them.   EMMA

On a spoiled son:
Sidney says anything, you know. He has always said what he chose of and to us all. Most families have such a member among them I believe . . . There is a some-one in most families privileged by superior abilities or spirits to say anything.   SANDITON

Nature versus nurture?:
It is a great deal more natural than one could wish, that a young man brought up by those who are proud, luxurious, and selfish, should be proud, luxurious, and selfish too.   EMMA

Blood may be thicker than water:
All the evil and good of their earliest years could be gone over again, and every former united pain and pleasure retraced with the fondest recollection. An advantage this, a strengthener of love, in which even the conjugal tie is beneath the fraternal. Children of the same family, the same blood, with the same first associations and habits, have some means of enjoyment in their power, which no subsequent connection can supply . . .   MANSFIELD PARK

But that does not make brothers good correspondents:

What strange creatures brothers are! You would not write to each other but upon the most urgent necessity in the world; and when obliged to take up the pen to say that such a horse is ill, or such a relation dead, it is done in the fewest possible words. You have but one style among you. I know it perfectly. Henry, who is in every other respect exactly what a brother should be, who loves me, consults me, confides in me, and will talk to me by the hour together, has never yet turned the page in a letter; and very often it is nothing more than, 'Dear Mary, I am just arrived. Bath seems full, and every thing as usual. Yours sincerely.' That is the true manly style; that is a complete brother's letter.

MANSFIELD PARK

An aunt defends her own:

Now that you are become an Aunt, you are a person of some consequence & must excite great Interest whatever you do. I have always maintained the importance of Aunts as much as possible . . .
(Letter to her niece Caroline Austen, 30 October 1815)

Lines left in a home-made needlework bag, given to her sister-in-law, January 1792 (recalled by her nephew J. Edward Austen-Leigh):

This little bag, I hope, will prove
    To be not vainly made;

For should you thread and needles want,
   It will afford you aid.

And, as we are about to part,
   'T will serve another end:
For, when you look upon this bag,
   You'll recollect your friend.

On the necessity of a room of one's own:
She could go there after any thing unpleasant below, and find immediate consolation in some pursuit, or some train of thought at hand. – Her plants, her books – of which she had been a collector, from the first hour of her commanding a shilling – her writing desk, and her works of charity and ingenuity, were all within her reach; – or if indisposed for employment, if nothing but musing would do, she could scarcely see an object in that room which had not an interesting remembrance connected with it. – Every thing was a friend, or bore her thoughts to a friend . . . The room was most dear to her, and she would not have changed its furniture for the handsomest in the house . . .

MANSFIELD PARK

Society

My idea of good company – is the company of clever, well-informed people, who have a great deal of conversation: that is what I call good company.

(PERSUASION)

On the importance of being important:
Every neighbourhood should have a great lady.

SANDITON

On the aristocratic virtues:
The Honourable John Yates . . . had not much to recommend him beyond habits of fashion and expense, and being the younger son of a lord with a tolerable independence . . .

MANSFIELD PARK

On the importance of keeping up appearances:
Those women are inexcusable who forget what is due to themselves and the opinion of the world.

LADY SUSAN

A woman's prerogative:
It is always the lady's right to decide on the degree of acquaintance.

EMMA

On the social function of the rich and well-connected:
Their coming gives a credit to our assemblies. The Osbornes being known to have been at the first ball, will dispose a great many people to attend the second. – It is more than they deserve, for in fact they add nothing to the pleasure of the evening, they come so late, and go so early; – but great people have always their charm.

THE WATSONS

On why rank matters:

$\mathcal{I}$ have laid Lady Sondes' case before Martha, who does not make the least objection to it, and is particularly pleased with the name Montresor. I do not agree with her there, but I like his rank very much, and always affix the ideas of strong sense and highly elegant manners to a general.

(Letter to her sister Cassandra, 27 December 1808)

Class counts for much, according to 'Catharine', written by Jane Austen when she was some sixteen years old:

$\mathcal{P}$erhaps he is come to rob the house – he comes in stile at least; and it will be some consolation for our losses to be robbed by a Gentleman in a Chaise and 4 . . .

On the need to balance appearance with economy:

$\mathcal{S}$ir Walter had at first thought more of London, but Mr Shepherd felt that he could not be trusted in London, and had been skilful enough to dissuade him from it, and make Bath preferred. It was a much safer place for a gentleman in his predicament: – he might there be important at comparatively little expense.

PERSUASION

On men's predilections for dining out:

$\mathcal{T}$here is, I believe, in many men, especially single men, such an inclination – such a passion for dining out – a dinner engagement is so high in the class of their pleasures, their employments, their dignities, almost their duties, that any thing gives way to it . . .

EMMA

On the child as social lubricant:
On every formal visit a child ought to be of the party, by way of provision for discourse. In the present case it took up ten minutes to determine whether the boy were most like his father or mother, and in what particular he resembled either, for of course every body differed, and every body was astonished at the opinion of the others. SENSE AND SENSIBILITY

A conversation round the piano on the art of small-talk:
'I certainly have not the talent which some people possess,' said Darcy, 'of conversing easily with those I have never seen before. I cannot catch their tone of conversation, or appear interested in their concerns, as I often see done.'

'My fingers,' said Elizabeth, 'do not move over this instrument in the masterly manner which I see so many women's do. They have not the same force or rapidity, and do not produce the same expression. But then I have always supposed it to be my own fault – because I would not take the trouble of practising. It is not that I do not believe *my* fingers as capable as any other woman's of superior execution.' PRIDE AND PREJUDICE

A mature man reasons with a giddy girl on the rival
attractions of town and country:

'You are not fond of the country.'

'Yes, I am. I have always lived there, and always been very happy. But certainly there is much more sameness in a country life than in a Bath life. One day in the country is exactly like another.'

'But then you spend your time so much more rationally in the country.'

'Do I?'

'Do you not?'

'I do not believe there is much difference.'

'Here you are in pursuit only of amusement all day long.'

'And so I am at home – only I do not find so much of it.'   NORTHANGER ABBEY

The curmudgeon's creed:

The sooner every party breaks up, the better.

EMMA

And a cheerier view:

One cannot have too large a party. A large party secures its own amusement.   EMMA

On the absurdity of amateur theatricals:

Now, Edmund, do not be disagreeable . . . Nobody

loves a play better than you do, or can have gone much farther to see one.'

'True, to see real acting, good hardened real acting; but I would hardly walk from this room to the next to look at the raw efforts of those who have not been bred to the trade, – a set of gentlemen and ladies, who have all the disadvantages of education and decorum to struggle through.'   MANSFIELD PARK

On dancing as a sign of marriageability:

He was quite young, wonderfully handsome, extremely agreeable, and to crown the whole, he meant to be at the next assembly with a large party. Nothing could be more delightful! To be fond of dancing was a certain step towards falling in love . . .

PRIDE AND PREJUDICE

And on dancing as an addiction:

It may be possible to do without dancing entirely. Instances have been known of young people passing many, many months successively, without being at any ball of any description, and no material injury accrue either to body or mind; – but when a beginning is made – when the felicities of rapid motion have once been, though slightly, felt – it must be a very heavy set that does not ask for more.   EMMA

On life as a ball:

I consider a country-dance as an emblem of marriage. Fidelity and complaisance are the principal duties of both . . .
NORTHANGER ABBEY

Dancing is not a spectator sport:

Pleasure in seeing dancing! – not I, indeed – I never look at it – I do not know who does. – Fine dancing, I believe, like virtue, must be its own reward.
EMMA

But still less, a harassed husband finds, is it something to be reported after the event:

Oh! my dear Mr Bennet . . . we have had a most delightful evening, a most excellent ball. I wish you had been there. Jane was so admired, nothing could be like it. Every body said how well she looked; and Mr Bingley thought her quite beautiful, and danced with her twice. Only think of *that* my dear; he actually danced with her twice; and she was the only creature in the room that he asked a second time. First of all, he asked Miss Lucas. I was so vexed to see him stand up with her; but, however, he did not admire her at all: indeed, nobody can, you know; and he seemed quite struck with Jane as she was going down the dance. So, he enquired who she was, and got introduced, and asked her for the two next. Then, the two third he danced with Miss King, and the two fourth with Maria

Lucas, and the two fifth with Jane again, and the two sixth with Lizzy, and the Boulanger – '

'If he had had any compassion for *me*,' cried her husband impatiently, 'he would not have danced half so much! For God's sake, say no more of his partners. Oh! That he had sprained his ankle in the first dance!'

PRIDE AND PREJUDICE

On the nature of 'naturalness', its affectation and reality.
A lady and a gentleman plan a picnic:

It is to be a morning scheme, you know . . . quite a simple thing. I shall wear a large bonnet, and bring one of my little baskets hanging on my arm. Here, – probably this basket with pink ribbon. Nothing can be more simple, you see . . . There is to be no form or parade – a sort of gipsy party. – We are to walk about your gardens, and gather the strawberries ourselves, and sit under trees; – and whatever else you may like to provide, it is to be all out of doors – a table spread in the shade, you know. Every thing as natural and simple as possible. Is not that your idea?'

'Not quite. My idea of the simple and the natural will be to have the table spread in the dining-room. The nature and the simplicity of gentlemen and ladies, with their servants and furniture, I think is best observed by meals within doors. When you are tired of eating strawberries in the garden, there shall be cold meat in the house.'

EMMA

A male view of the social code:

'A man,' said he, 'must have a very good opinion of himself when he asks people to leave their own fireside, and encounter such a day as this, for the sake of coming to see him. He must think himself a most agreeable fellow; I could not do such a thing. It is the greatest absurdity – Actually snowing at this moment! – The folly of not allowing people to be comfortable at home – and the folly of people's not staying comfortably at home when they can! If we were obliged to go out on such an evening as this, by any call of duty or business, what a hardship we should deem it; – and here we are, probably with rather thinner clothing than usual, setting forward voluntarily, without excuse, in defiance of the voice of nature, which tells man, in every thing given to his view or his feelings, to stay at home himself, and keep all under shelter that he can; – here are we setting forward to spend five dull hours in another man's house, with nothing to say or to hear that was not said and heard yesterday, and may not be said and heard again to-morrow. Going in dismal weather, to return probably in worse; – four horses and four servants taken out for nothing but to convey five idle, shivering creatures into colder rooms and worse company than they might have had at home.'

EMMA

The worst social gaffe:

Poor Mrs C. Milles, that she should die on a wrong

day at last, after being about it so long! – It was unlucky that the Goodnestone Party could not meet you, & I hope her friendly, obliging, social Spirit, which delighted in drawing people together, was not conscious of the division and disappointment she was occasioning.

(Letter to her niece Fanny Knight, 13 March 1817)

A Lady's Accomplishments

*It was much easier to chat than to study: much pleasanter
to let her imagination range and work . . . than
to be labouring to enlarge her comprehension or exercise it
on sober facts.*

(EMMA)

Ignorance is bliss:

*W*hen people wish to attach, they should always be ignorant. To come with a well-informed mind is to come with an ability of administering to the vanity of others, which a sensible person would always wish to avoid. A woman, especially, if she have the misfortune of knowing any thing, should conceal it as well as she can.

NORTHANGER ABBEY

No need for idiocy; ignorance will do:

*T*he advantages of folly in a beautiful girl have been already set forth . . . I will only add in justice to men, that though to the larger and more trifling part of the sex, imbecility in females is a great enhancement of their personal charms, there is a portion of them too reasonable and too well informed themselves to desire any thing more in woman than ignorance.

NORTHANGER ABBEY

A fashionable matron:

*T*o the education of her daughters, Lady Bertram paid not the smallest attention. She had not time for such cares. She was a woman who spent her days in sitting nicely dressed on a sofa, doing some long piece of needlework, of little use and no beauty, thinking more of her pug than her children, but very indulgent to the latter, when it did not put herself to inconvenience . . . Had she possessed greater leisure for the service of her girls, she would probably have supposed it unnecessary, for they were under the care of a governess, with proper masters, and could want nothing more.

MANSFIELD PARK

A woman sets out her accomplishments:

Miss Crawford's attractions did not lessen. The harp arrived, and rather added to her beauty, wit, and good humour, for she played with the greatest obligingness, with an expression and taste which were peculiarly becoming, and there was something clever to be said at the close of every air . . . A young woman, pretty, lively, with a harp as elegant as herself; and both placed near a window, cut down to the ground, and opening on a little lawn, surrounded by shrubs in the rich foliage of summer, was enough to catch any man's heart. The season, the scene, the air, were all favourable to tenderness and sentiment. Mrs Grant and her tambour frame were not without their use; it was all in harmony; and as every thing will turn to account when love is once set going, even the sandwich tray, and Dr Grant doing the honours of it, were worth looking at.

MANSFIELD PARK

The case against feminine accomplishments:

Not that I am an advocate for the prevailing fashion of acquiring a perfect knowledge in all the languages, arts and sciences; it is throwing time away; to be mistress of

French, Italian, German, music, singing, drawing, etc., will gain a woman some applause, but will not add one lover to her list. Grace and manner after all are of the greatest importance. I do not mean therefore that Frederica's acquirements should be more than superficial, and I flatter myself that she will not remain long enough at school to understand anything thoroughly.

LADY SUSAN

And an opposing view:
Give a girl an education, and introduce her properly into the world, and ten to one but she has the means of settling well, without farther expenses to anybody.

MANSFIELD PARK

On unpretentiousness in education:
Mrs Goddard was the mistress of a School – not of a seminary, or an establishment, or any thing which professed, in long sentences of refined nonsense, to combine liberal acquirements with elegant morality upon new principles and new systems – and where young ladies for enormous pay might be screwed out of health and into vanity – but a real, honest, old-fashioned Boarding-school, where a reasonable quantity of accomplishments were sold at a reasonable price, and where girls might be sent to be out of the way and scramble themselves into a little education, without any danger of coming back prodigies.

EMMA

Small mercies in a schoolteacher:

I hope I have acquitted myself pretty well; but having a very reasonable Lady to deal with, one who only required a *tolerable* temper, my office was not difficult. – Were I going to send a girl to school I would send her to this person; to be rational in anything is great praise, especially in the ignorant class of school mistresses . . .

(Letter to her sister Cassandra, 8 April 1805)

And pity the authors of history books . . . :

To be at so much trouble in filling great volumes, which . . . nobody would willingly look into, to be labouring only for the torment of little boys and girls, always struck me as a hard fate.

NORTHANGER ABBEY

On the dangers of ladylike accomplishment without adult understanding, the sixteen-year-old author writes warningly, in 'Catharine':

Miss Stanley had been attended by the most capital Masters from the time of her being six years old to the last Spring, which comprehending a period of twelve Years had been dedicated to the acquirement of Accomplishments which were now to be displayed and in a few Years entirely neglected. She was elegant in her appearance, rather handsome, and naturally not deficient in Abilities; but those Years which ought to have been spent in the attainment of useful knowledge and Mental Improvement, had been all bestowed in learning Drawing, Italian and Music, more especially the latter, and she now united to these Accomplishments, an Understanding unimproved by reading and a Mind totally devoid either of Taste or Judgement. Her temper was by Nature good, but unassisted by reflection, she had neither patience under Disappointment, nor could sacrifice her own inclinations to promote the happiness of others. All her Ideas were towards the Elegance of her appearance, the fashion of her dress, and the Admiration she wished them to excite. She professed a love of Books without reading, was Lively without Wit, and generally Good humoured without Merit.

On the danger of being too talented to try:
Her many beginnings were displayed. Miniatures, half-lengths, whole lengths, pencil, crayon, and water-colours had been all tried in turn. She had always wanted to do everything, and had made more progress both in drawing and music than many might have done with so little labour as she would ever submit to. She played and sang; – and drew in almost every style; but steadiness had always been wanting; and in nothing had she approached the degree of excellence which she would have been glad to command, and ought not to have failed of.   EMMA

On the perils of praise too easily won:
She was not much deceived as to her own skill either as an artist or a musician, but she was not unwilling to have others deceived, or sorry to know her reputation for accomplishment often higher than it deserved.

EMMA

On writing as a feminine gift – a male perspective:
'As far as I have had opportunity of judging, it appears to me that the usual style of letter-writing among women is faultless, except in three particulars.'

'And what are they?'

'A general deficiency of subject, a total inattention to stops, and a very frequent ignorance of grammar.'

NORTHANGER ABBEY

The same man on the female intellect:
No one can think more highly of the understanding of women than I do. In my opinion, nature has given them so much, that they never find it necessary to use more than half.

NORTHANGER ABBEY

On the uses of articulacy:
If I am vain of anything, it is of my eloquence. Consideration and esteem as surely follow command of language, as admiration waits upon beauty.

LADY SUSAN

A flibbertigibbet:

Emma has been meaning to read more ever since she was twelve years old. I have seen a great many lists of her drawing up at various times of books that she meant to read regularly through – and very good lists they were – very well chosen, and very neatly arranged – sometimes alphabetically, and sometimes by some other rule. The list she drew up when only fourteen – I remember thinking it did her judgment so much credit, that I preserved it some time; and I dare say she may have made out a very good list now. But I have done with expecting any course of steady reading from Emma. She will never submit to any thing requiring industry and patience, and a subjection of the fancy to the understanding.   EMMA

On the importance of grown-up example to the moral education of the young – something Jane Austen already understood clearly when she wrote the cheery mock-novel 'Jack and Alice' at the age of twelve:

Miss Dickins was an excellent Governess. She instructed me in the Paths of Virtue; under her tuition I daily became more amiable, and might perhaps by this time have nearly attained perfection, had not my worthy Preceptoress been torn from my arms, e'er I had attained my seventeenth year. I never shall forget her last words. "My dear Kitty," she said, "good night t'ye." I never saw her afterwards,' continued Lady Williams wiping her eyes. 'She eloped with the Butler the same night.'

Some Characters Observed

I hope I never ridicule what is wise or good. Follies and nonsense, whims and inconsistencies do divert me, I own, and I laugh at them whenever I can.
(PRIDE AND PREJUDICE)

A silly woman, at work and play:

The business of her life was to get her daughters married; its solace was visiting and news.

PRIDE AND PREJUDICE

A fine fellow:

His conversation, or rather talk, began and ended with himself and his own concerns. He told her of horses which he had bought for a trifle and sold for incredible sums; of racing matches, in which his judgment had infallibly foretold the winner; of shooting parties, in which he had killed more birds (though without having one good shot) than all his companions together; and described to her some famous day's sport, with the fox-hounds, in which his foresight and skill in directing the dogs had repaired the mistakes of the most experienced huntsman, and in which the boldness of his riding, though it had never endangered his own life for a moment, had been constantly leading others into difficulties, which he calmly concluded had broken the necks of many.

NORTHANGER ABBEY

A happy woman:

She had never boasted either beauty or cleverness. Her youth had passed without distinction, and her middle of life was devoted to the care of a failing mother, and the endeavour to make a small income go as far as possible. And yet she was a happy woman, and a woman whom no one named without good-will. It was her own universal good-will and contented temper which worked such wonders. She loved every body, was interested in every body's happiness, quick-sighted to every body's merits; thought herself a most fortunate creature, and surrounded with blessings in such an excellent mother and so many good neighbours and friends, and a home that wanted for nothing. The simplicity and cheerfulness of her nature, her contented and grateful spirit, were a recommendation to every body and a mine of felicity to herself. She was a great talker upon little matters . . . full of trivial communications and harmless gossip.

EMMA

A flirt of genius:

My dear sister,

I congratulate you and Mr Vernon on being about to receive into your family, the most accomplished coquette in England. As a very distinguished flirt, I have always been taught to consider her; but it has lately fallen in my way to hear some particulars of her conduct at Langford, which prove that she does not confine herself to that sort of honest flirtation which satisfies most people, but aspires to the more delicious gratification of making a whole family miserable . . . What a woman she must be! I long to see her, and shall certainly accept your kind invitation, that I may form some idea of those bewitching powers which can do so much – engaging at the same time and in the same house the affections of two men who were neither of them at liberty to bestow them – and all this, without the charm of youth.   LADY SUSAN

An eligible bachelor?:
If this man had not twelve thousand a year, he would be a very stupid fellow.   MANSFIELD PARK

A pompous young lady put down:
'I should like balls infinitely better,' she replied, 'if they were carried on in a different manner; but there is something insufferably tedious in the usual process of such a meeting. It would surely be much more rational if conversation instead of dancing made the order of the day.'

'Much more rational, my dear Caroline, I dare say, but it would not be near so much like a ball.'
                                            PRIDE AND PREJUDICE

On a family that is going up in the world:
The Musgroves, like their houses, were in a state of alteration, perhaps of improvement. The father and mother were in the old English style, and the young people in the new. Mr and Mrs Musgrove were a very good sort of people; friendly and hospitable, not much educated, and not at all elegant. Their children had

more modern minds and manners.

PERSUASION

On an attention-seeking invalid:
He knew her illnesses; they never occurred but for her own convenience.   EMMA

A health-food freak – and his hypocrisies:
'Then I will help myself,' said he. – 'A large dish of rather weak cocoa every evening, agrees with me better than any thing.'

It struck her, however, as he poured out this rather weak cocoa, that it came forth in a very fine, dark coloured stream – and at the same moment, his sisters both crying out – 'Oh! Arthur, you get your cocoa stronger and stronger every evening' – with Arthur's somewhat conscious reply of ''Tis rather stronger than it should be tonight' – convinced her that Arthur was by no means so fond of being starved as they could desire, or as he felt proper himself. – He was certainly very happy to turn the conversation on dry toast, and hear no more of his sisters.

'I hope you will eat some of this toast,' said he, 'I reckon myself a very good toaster; I never burn my toasts – I never put them too near the fire at first – and yet, you see, there is not a corner but what is well browned. – I hope you like dry toast.'

'With a reasonable quantity of butter spread over

it, very much – ' said Charlotte – 'but not otherwise. – '

'No more do I' – said he exceedingly pleased – 'We think quite alike there. – So far from dry toast being wholesome, *I* think it a very bad thing for the stomach. Without a little butter to soften it, it hurts the coats of the stomach. I am sure it does . . . It irritates and acts like a nutmeg grater.'
                                                    SANDITON

A parvenue denounces a rival:

I have quite a horror of upstarts. Maple Grove has given me a thorough disgust to people of that sort; for there is a family in that neighbourhood who are such an annoyance to my brother and sister from the airs they give themselves! . . . People of the name of Tupman, very lately settled here, and encumbered with many low connections, but giving themselves immense airs, and expecting to be on a footing with the old established families. A year and a half is the very utmost that they can have lived at West Hall; and how they got their fortune nobody knows. They came from Birmingham, which is not a place to promise much, you know . . . One has not great hopes from Birmingham. I always say there is something direful in the sound: but nothing more is positively known of the Tupmans, though a good many things I assure you are suspected; and yet by their manners they evidently think themselves equal even to my brother, Mr Suckling, who happens to be one of their nearest neighbours. It is

infinitely too bad. Mr Suckling, who has been eleven
years a resident at Maple Grove, and whose father had
it before him – I believe, at least – I am almost sure that
old Mr Suckling had completed the purchase before his
death.'   EMMA

*On young ladies who are too smart for their own, or
anybody else's, good:*

As they joined to beauty and brilliant acquirements, a
manner naturally easy, and carefully formed to general
civility and obligingness, they possessed its favour as
well as its admiration. Their vanity was in such good
order, that they seemed to be quite free from it, and
gave themselves no airs; while the praises attending such
behaviour . . . served to strengthen them in believing
they had no faults.   MANSFIELD PARK

A busybody is outmanoeuvred:

She was vexed by the *manner* of his return. It had left
her nothing to do. Instead of being sent for out of the
room, and seeing him first, and having to spread the
happy news through the house, Sir Thomas . . . had
sought no confidant but the butler, and had been
following him almost instantaneously into the drawing-
room. Mrs Norris felt herself defrauded of an office on
which she had always depended, whether his arrival or
his death were to be the thing unfolded; and was now
trying to be in a bustle without having any thing to

bustle about; and labouring to be important where nothing was wanted but tranquillity and silence. Would Sir Thomas have consented to eat, she might have gone to the house-keeper with troublesome directions, and insulted the footmen with injunctions of dispatch; but Sir Thomas resolutely declined all dinner; he would take nothing, nothing till tea came – he would rather wait for tea. Still Mrs Norris was at intervals urging something different, and in the most interesting moment of his passage to England, when the alarm of a French privateer was at the height, she burst through his recital with the proposal of soup. 'Sure, my dear Sir Thomas, a basin of soup would be a much better thing for you than tea. Do have a basin of soup.'

MANSFIELD PARK

On a silly, but good-hearted woman:
She is a woman that one may, that one *must* laugh at; but that one would not wish to slight.

EMMA

On a charming young man:
Mr Wickham is blessed with such happy manners as may ensure his *making* friends – whether he may be equally capable of *retaining* them, is less certain.

PRIDE AND PREJUDICE

On a class one snob:

Sir Walter Elliot, of Kellynch-hall, in Somersetshire, was a man who, for his own amusement, never took up any book but the Baronetage; there he found occupation for an idle hour, and consolation in a distressed one; there his faculties were roused into admiration and respect, by contemplating the limited remnant of the earliest patents; there any unwelcome sensations, arising from domestic affairs, changed naturally into pity and contempt, as he turned over the almost endless creations of the last century – and there, if every other leaf were powerless, he could read his own history with an interest which never failed . . .

PERSUASION

On petticoats and propriety:

You will find Captain —— a very respectable, well-meaning man, without much manner, his wife and sister all good humour and obligingness, and I hope (since the fashion allows it) with rather longer petticoats than last year.

(Letter to unknown recipient, May 1817)

A decidedly irreverent view of the reverend vocation:

Oh! no doubt he is very sincere in preferring an income ready made, to the trouble of working for one; and has the best intentions of doing nothing at all the rest of his days but eat, drink, and grow fat. It is indolence . . . indeed. Indolence and love of ease – a want of all laudable ambition, of taste for good company, or of inclination to take the trouble of being agreeable, which make men clergymen. A clergyman has nothing to do but to be slovenly and selfish – read the newspaper, watch the weather and quarrel with his wife. His curate does all the work, and the business of his own life is to dine. MANSFIELD PARK

And a woman who knows her own worth:
I always deserve the best treatment, because I never put up with any other . . . EMMA

Human Nature

Nobody ever feels or acts, suffers or enjoys, as one expects.
(Letter to her sister Cassandra, 30 June 1808)

On the incomprehensibility of our fellow beings:
One half of the world cannot understand the pleasures of the other.
EMMA

On energy and inclination:
Nothing ever fatigues me, but doing what I do not like.
MANSFIELD PARK

Arguments of convenience:
How quick come the reasons for approving what we like!
PERSUASION

A disagreeable law:
I am afraid . . . that the pleasantness of an employment does not always evince its propriety.
SENSE AND SENSIBILITY

It is easier to preach than to practise:
Like many other great moralists and preachers, she had been eloquent on a point in which her own conduct would ill bear examination.

PERSUASION

On the duty of mutual amusement:
For what do we live, but to make sport for our neighbours, and laugh at them in our turn?
PRIDE AND PREJUDICE

Manners makyth man (though a bit of property always helps):

Tom Bertram must have been thought pleasant . . . he was the sort of young man to be generally liked, his agreeableness was of the kind to be oftener found agreeable than some endowments of a higher stamp, for he had easy manners, excellent spirits, a large acquaintance, and a great deal to say; and the reversion of Mansfield Park, and a baronetcy, did no harm to all this.

MANSFIELD PARK

Presentation is all:

There is hardly any personal defect . . . which an agreeable manner might not gradually reconcile one to.

PERSUASION

Good feelings are better than brains:

There is no charm equal to tenderness of heart . . . There is nothing to be compared to it. Warmth and tenderness of heart, with an affectionate, open manner, will beat all the clearness of head in the world, for attraction.

EMMA

On truth and its elusiveness:

Seldom, very seldom, does complete truth belong to any human disclosure; seldom can it happen that something is not a little disguised, or a little mistaken . . .

EMMA

On the successful conclusion of a gold-digger's campaign:
The affair, and the prosperity which crowned it, there-fore, may be held forth as a most encouraging instance of what an earnest, an unceasing attention to self-interest, however its progress may be apparently obstructed, will do in securing every advantage of fortune, with no other sacrifice than that of time and conscience. SENSE AND SENSIBILITY

Moments of crisis, moments of discovery:
Every body's heart is open, you know, when they have recently escaped from severe pain, or are recovering the blessing of health. PERSUASION

No use crying over spilt milk:
You must learn some of my philosophy. Think only of the past as its remembrance gives you pleasure.
PRIDE AND PREJUDICE

No experience is ever wasted:
When pain is over, the remembrance of it often becomes a pleasure. PERSUASION

Reflections on time, and on the tricks the memory plays, as inspired by gazing at a growing garden:
Every time I come into this shrubbery I am more struck with its growth and beauty. Three years ago, this

was nothing but a rough hedgerow along the upper side of the field, never thought of as any thing, or capable of becoming any thing; and now it is converted into a walk, and it would be difficult to say whether most valuable as a convenience or an ornament; and perhaps in another three years we may be forgetting – almost forgetting what it was before. How wonderful, how very wonderful the operations of time, and the changes of the human mind! . . . If any one faculty of our nature may be called *more* wonderful than the rest, I do think it is memory. There seems something more speakingly incomprehensible in the powers, the failures, the inequalities of memory, than in any other of our intelligences. The memory is sometimes so retentive, so serviceable, so obedient – at others, so bewildered and so weak – and at others again, so tyrannic, so beyond control! – We are to be sure a miracle every way – but our powers of recollecting and of forgetting, do seem peculiarly past finding out.   Mansfield Park

On being on top:
[*It* is always] a great deal better to chuse than to be chosen, to excite gratitude than to feel it.

Emma

All praise is relative:
To look *almost* pretty, is an acquisition of higher delight to a girl who has been looking plain the first fifteen

years of her life, than a beauty from her cradle can ever receive.   NORTHANGER ABBEY

On the need for humility:
Vanity working on a weak head, produces every sort of mischief. Nothing so easy as for a young lady to raise her expectations too high.   EMMA

On the difficulty we have in understanding our own insignificance:
Anne had not wanted this visit to Uppercross, to learn that a removal from one set of people to another, though at a distance of only three miles, will often include a total change of conversation, opinion, and idea. She had never been staying there before, without being struck by it, or without wishing that other Elliots could have her advantage in seeing how unknown, or unconsidered there, were the affairs which at Kellynch-hall were treated as of such general publicity and pervading interest; yet, with all this experience, she believed she must now submit to feel that another lesson, in the art of knowing our own nothingness beyond our own circle, was become necessary for her . . .
          PERSUASION

On the necessity to seize the moment:
How often is happiness destroyed by preparation, foolish preparation!   EMMA

On the need for firmness and decision:
It is the worst evil of too yielding and indecisive a character, that no influence over it can be depended on. —You are never sure of a good impression being durable. Every body may sway it . . .   PERSUASION

Deviousness discouraged:
How much I love every thing that is decided and open!   EMMA

A liar's complaint:
Facts are such horrid things!

LADY SUSAN

On the importance of being honest:
That upright integrity, that strict adherence to truth and principle, that disdain of trick and littleness, which a man should display in every transaction of his life.

EMMA

On the evils of intrigue:
Mystery; Finesse — how they pervert the understanding! . . . does not every thing serve to prove more and more the beauty of truth and sincerity in all our dealings with each other?   EMMA

*On the fickleness of folk, as revealed in the sad case of
the death of the local haberdasher:*

The Neighbourhood have quite recovered the death
of Mrs Rider – so much so, that I think they are rather
rejoiced at it now; her things were so very dear! – &
Mrs Rogers is to be all that is desirable. Not even Death
itself can fix the friendship of the World.

(Letter to her sister Cassandra, 21 January 1801)

A surprising suggestion:

Surprises are foolish things. The pleasure is not
enhanced, and the inconvenience is often considerable.

EMMA

Not just men are swayed by female charms:

Beauty, sweetness, poverty and dependence, do not
want the imagination of a man to operate upon. With
due exceptions – woman feels for woman very promptly
and compassionately.

SANDITON

Fatness and feeling, an unpleasant observation:

Personal size and mental sorrow have certainly no
necessary proportions. A large bulky figure has as good
a right to be in deep affliction, as the most graceful set
of limbs in the world. But, fair or not fair, there are un-
becoming conjunctions, which reason will patronise in
vain, – which taste cannot tolerate, – which ridicule
will seize.

PERSUASION

Changes in fashion, foibles and fever:
What is become of all the Shyness in the World? –
Moral as well as Natural Diseases disappear in the
progress of time, & new ones take their place. – Shyness
& the Sweating Sickness have given way to Confidence
& Paralytic Complaints.

(Letter to her sister Cassandra, 8 February 1807)

*On nurses, and their incomparable insights into all
human life:*
Such varieties of human nature as they are in the habit
of witnessing! And it is not merely in its follies, that
they are well read; for they see it occasionally under
every circumstance that can be most interesting or
affecting. What instances must pass before them of ardent, disinterested, self-denying attachment, of heroism,
fortitude, patience, resignation – of all the conflicts and
all the sacrifices that ennoble us most. A sick chamber
may often furnish the worth of volumes.

PERSUASION

On the horrors of war:
How horrible it is to have so many people killed! –
And what a blessing that one cares for none of them!

(Letter to her sister Cassandra, 31 May 1811)

On the inherent dignity of genuine emotion:
Her tears fell abundantly – but her grief was so truly

artless, that no dignity could have made it more respectable . . .   EMMA

On the joy of having been talked about:
No one can withstand the charm of such a mystery. To have been described long ago to a recent acquaintance, by nameless people, is irresistible . . .

PERSUASION

On the (unfair) advantages of optimism:
A sanguine temper, though for ever expecting more good than occurs, does not always pay for its hopes by any proportionate depression. It soon flies over the present failure, and begins to hope again.

EMMA

All the world loves a talking-point:
Human nature is so well disposed towards those who are in interesting situations, that a young person, who either marries or dies, is sure of being kindly spoken of.

EMMA

On self-indulgence in grief:
Elinor saw, with concern, the excess of her sister's sensibility; but by Mrs Dashwood it was valued and cherished. They encouraged each other now in the violence of their affliction. The agony of grief which

overpowered them at first, was voluntarily renewed, was sought for, was created again and again. They gave themselves up wholly to their sorrow, seeking increase of wretchedness in every reflection that could afford it, and resolved against ever admitting consolation in future. SENSE AND SENSIBILITY

On the dangers of an excess of sensibility, from 'Love and Freindship', written when Jane Austen was fourteen:

'My beloved Laura' (said she to me a few Hours before she died) 'take warning from my unhappy End and avoid the imprudent conduct which has occasioned it . . . Beware of fainting-fits . . . Though at the time they may be refreshing and Agreable yet believe me they will in the end, if too often repeated and at improper seasons, prove destructive to your Constitution . . . My fate will teach you this . . . One fatal swoon has cost me my Life . . . Beware of swoons, Dear Laura . . . A frenzy fit is not one quarter so pernicious; it is an exercise to the Body and if not too violent, is I dare say conducive to Health in its consequences – Run mad as often as you chuse; but do not faint . . .'

Poverty as a crime:

People get so horridly poor & economical in this part of the World, that I have no patience with them. – Kent

is the only place for happiness, Everybody is rich
there . . .

(Letter to her sister Cassandra, 18 December 1798)

On the limits of economy:
There are some circumstances which even *women*
cannot control. – Female economy will do a great deal
. . . but it cannot turn a small income into a large one.
THE WATSONS

Guineas are good for you:
She looks remarkably well (legacies are very
wholesome diet) . . .

(Letter to her sister Cassandra, 15 June 1808)

Another female failing – a male view:
A woman should never be trusted with money.
THE WATSONS

*What has wealth to do with happiness? asks one sister
of another:*
'Grandeur has but little,' said Elinor, 'but wealth has
much to do with it.'

'Elinor, for shame!' said Marianne; 'money can
only give happiness where there is nothing else to give
it. Beyond a competence, it can afford no real satisfaction, as far as mere self is concerned.'

'Perhaps,' said Elinor, smiling, 'we may come to

the same point. *Your* competence and *my* wealth are very much alike, I dare say; and without them, as the world goes now, we shall both agree that every kind of external comfort must be wanting. Your ideas are only more noble than mine. Come, what is your competence?'

'About eighteen hundred or two thousand a-year; not more than *that*.'

Elinor laughed. '*Two* thousand a-year! *One* is my wealth! I guessed how it would end.'

SENSE AND SENSIBILITY

A golden rule:
The rich are always respectable.
(Letter to her sister Cassandra, 20 June 1808)

The Written Word

I think I may boast myself to be, with all possible vanity, the most unlearned and uninformed female who ever dared to be an authoress.
(Letter to James Stanier Clarke, 11 December 1815)

A novelist writes:

The person, be it gentleman or lady, who has not pleasure in a good novel, must be intolerably stupid.

NORTHANGER ABBEY

A novelist stands by her craft:

'And what are you reading, Miss——?''Oh! It is only a novel!' replies the young lady; while she lays down her book with affected indifference, or momentary shame . . . in short, only some work in which the greatest powers of the mind are displayed, in which the most thorough knowledge of human nature, the happiest delineation of its varieties, the liveliest effusions of wit and humour are conveyed to the world in the best chosen language.

NORTHANGER ABBEY

On the solace of reading:

The employment of mind, the dissipation of unpleasant ideas which only reading could produce, made her thankfully turn to a book.

THE WATSONS

Though the happy ending seems impossible, there's no fooling the experienced romance-reader!:

The anxiety, which in this state of their attachment must be the portion of Henry and Catherine, and of all who loved either, as to its final event, can hardly extend, I fear, to the bosom of my readers, who will see in the tell-tale compression of the pages before them, that we are all hastening together to perfect felicity. The means by which their early marriage was effected can be the only doubt . . .   NORTHANGER ABBEY

On an intimidating reader:
I am gratified by her having pleasure in what I write – but I wish the knowledge of my being exposed to her discerning Criticism, may not hurt my stile, by inducing too great a solicitude. I begin already to weigh my words and sentences more than I did, and am looking about for a sentiment, an illustration or a metaphor in every corner of the room.

(Letter to her sister Cassandra, 24 January 1809)

On reading the competition:
[I] am always half afraid of finding a clever novel *too clever* – and of finding my own story and my own people all forestalled.

(Letter to Cassandra, 30 April 1811)

On the absurd 'art' of letter-writing:
I have now attained the true art of letter-writing, which we are always told, is to express on paper exactly what one would say to the same person by word of mouth; I have been talking to you almost as fast as I could the whole of this letter.

(Letter to Cassandra, 3 January 1801)

On the need for perfectionism:
An artist cannot do anything slovenly.

> (Letter to Cassandra, 25 November 1798)

On the distractions of housework:
Composition seems to me Impossible, with a head full of Joints of Mutton & doses of rhubarb.

> (Letter to Cassandra, 8 September 1816)

In a series of letters to her niece, Anna Austen, Jane offered some tips in the novelist's art, to a young would-be writer. First, the all-important injunction to 'write about what you know':
We think you had better not leave England. Let the Portmans go to Ireland, but as you know nothing of the Manners there, you had better not go with them. You will be in danger of giving false representations. Stick to Bath & the Foresters.

> (10 August 1814)

Next there's a hint on practical plotting:
Your aunt C. does not like desultory novels, & is rather fearful yours will be too much so, that there will be too frequent a change from one set of people to another, & that circumstances will be sometimes introduced of apparent consequence, which will lead to nothing. – It will not be so great an objection to *me*, if it does. I allow much more Latitude than she does – & think Nature

and Spirit cover many sins of a wandering story – and People in general do not care so much about it – for your comfort. (10 August 1814)

On the need for consistency in characterisation:
I like your Susan very much indeed, she is a sweet creature, her playfulness of fancy is very delightful. I like her as she is *now* exceedingly, but I am not so well satisfied with her behaviour to George R. At first she seemed all over attachment & feeling, & afterwards to have none at all; she is so extremely composed at the Ball, & so well-satisfied apparently with Mr Morgan. She seems to have changed her Character.

(9 September 1814)

And then there's the need to find a situation that works, and the right sort of character-chemistry:
You are now collecting your People delightfully, getting them exactly into such a spot as is the delight of my life; – 3 or 4 families in a Country Village is the very thing to work on – & I hope you will write a great deal more, & make full use of them while they are so very favourably arranged. You are but *now* coming to the heart & beauty of your book . . .

(9 September 1814)

On the need to avoid clichés:

Henry Mellish I am afraid will be too much in the common Novel style – a handsome, amiable, unexceptionable Young Man (such as do not much abound in real Life) desperately in Love, & all in vain . . . Devereaux Forester's being ruined by his Vanity is extremely good; but I wish you would not let him plunge into a 'vortex of Dissipation.' I do not object to the Thing, but I cannot bear the expression; – it is such thorough novel slang – and so old, that I dare say Adam met with it in the first novel he opened . . .

(28 September 1814)

For a younger niece, Caroline Austen, there'd be a deliciously backhanded compliment ('I wish I could finish Stories as fast as you can') and some enjoyably preposterous literary criticism:

I am much obliged to you for the sight of Olivia, & think you have done for her very well; but the good for nothing Father, who was the real author of all her Faults and Sufferings, should not escape unpunished. I hope *he* hung himself, or took the surname of *Bone* or underwent some direful penance or other . . .

(Letter to Caroline Austen, 6 December 1815)

Only twelve when her Aunt Jane died, Caroline was still, she would recall many years afterwards, the recipient of some invaluable advice. Writing had to be kept in its place, her aunt insisted. Reading was at least as important for both the growing girl and the would-be novelist:

As I grew older, my aunt would talk to me more seriously of my reading and my amusements. I had taken early to writing verses, and stories, and I am sorry to think how I troubled her with reading them. She was very kind about it, and always had some praise to bestow, but at last she warned me against spending too much time upon them. She said – how well I recollect it! – that she knew writing stories was a great amusement, and *she* thought a harmless one, though many people, she was aware, thought otherwise; but that at my age it would be bad for me to be much taken up with my own compositions. Later still . . . she sent me a message to this effect, that if I would take her advice I should cease writing till I was sixteen; that she had herself often wished she had read more, and written less in the corresponding years of her own life.

On the rules of writerly solidarity, and the flagrant breach represented by the Waverley Novels:

Walter Scott has no business to write novels, especially good ones. – It is not fair. – He has Fame and Profit enough as a Poet, and should not be taking the bread out of other people's mouths.

(Letter to her niece Anna Austen, 28 September 1814)

Jane showed a clear-sighted sense of her own interests and limitations – as well as a diplomatically expressed firmness in refusing to be bullied – in her response to the suggestion from the Prince Regent's Private Secretary that she write a 'historical romance, illustrative of the history of the August House of Cobourg':

You are very very kind in your hints as to the sort of composition which might recommend me at present, and I am fully sensible that an historical romance, founded on the House of Saxe Cobourg, might be much more to the purpose of profit or popularity than such pictures of domestic life in country villages as I deal in. But I could no more write a romance than an epic poem. I could not sit seriously down to write a serious romance under any other motive than to save my life; and if it were indispensable for me to keep it up and never relax into laughing at myself or other people, I am sure I should be hung before I had finished the first chapter. No, I must keep to my own style and go on in my own way; and though I may never succeed again in that, I am convinced that I should totally fail in any other.

(Letter to James Stanier Clarke, 1 April 1816)

Jane Austen was the recipient of a good deal of well-meaning advice from those who thought they knew what she should be writing her next novel about. In playful mood, she collected some of these suggestions together to produce a single 'Plan of a novel according to hints from various quarters'.

Scene to be in the Country, Heroine the Daughter of a Clergyman . . . He, the most excellent Man that can be imagined, perfect in Character, Temper and Manners – without the smallest drawback or peculiarity to prevent his being the most delightful companion to his Daughter from one year's end to the other. – Heroine a faultless character herself –, perfectly good, with much tenderness and sentiment, and not the least Wit . . . Book to open with the description of Father and Daughter – who are to converse in long speeches, elegant Language – and a tone of high, serious sentiment . . . From this outset, the Story will proceed, and contain a striking variety of adventures. Heroine and her Father never above a fortnight together in one place, *he* being driven from his Curacy by the vile arts of some totally unprincipled and heartless young Man, desperately in love with the Heroine, and pursuing her with unrelenting passion – no sooner settled in one Country of Europe than they are necessitated to quit it and retire to another – always making new acquaintance, and always obliged to leave them. – This will of course exhibit a wide variety of Characters –

But there will be no mixture; the scene will be for ever shifting from one Set of People to another – but all the Good will be unexceptionable in every respect – and there will be no foibles or weaknesses but with the Wicked, who will be completely depraved and infamous, hardly a resemblance of Humanity left in them. – Early in her career, in the progress of her first removals, Heroine must meet with the Hero – all perfection of course – and only prevented from paying his addresses to her by some excess of refinement. – Wherever she goes, somebody falls in love with her, and she receives repeated offers of Marriage . . . Often carried away by the anti-hero, but rescued either by her Father or the Hero – often reduced to support herself and her Father by her Talents, and work for her Bread; – continually cheated and defrauded of her hire, worn down to a Skeleton, and now and then starved to death – . At last, hunted out of civilised Society, denied the poor Shelter of the humblest Cottage, they are compelled to retreat into Kamschatka where the poor Father, quite worn down, finding his end approaching, throws himself on the Ground, and after 4 or 5 hours of tender advice and parental Admonition to his miserable Child, expires in a fine burst of Literary Enthusiasm . . . Heroine inconsolable for some time – but afterwards crawls back towards her former Country – having at least 20 narrow escapes of falling into the hands of Anti-hero – and at last in the very nick of time, turning a corner to avoid him, runs into the arms of the Hero himself, who having just shaken off the scruples which fetter'd him before, was at the very moment setting off in pursuit of her. – The Tenderest and completest Eclaircissement takes place, and they are happily united. – Throughout the whole work, Heroine to be in the most elegant Society and living in high style.

Not, one assumes, a Jane Austen reader – a sublimely stupid young intellectual:

The novels which I approve are such as display human nature with grandeur – such as show her in the sublimities of intense feeling – such as exhibit the progress of strong passion from the first germ of incipient susceptibility to the utmost energies of reason half-dethroned, – where we see the strong spark of woman's captivations elicit such fire in the soul of man as leads him – (though at the risk of some aberration from the strict line of primitive obligations) – to hazard all, dare all, achieve all, to obtain her. – Such are the works which I peruse with delight, and I hope I may say, with amelioration. They hold forth the most splendid portraitures of high conceptions, unbounded views, illimitable ardour, indomptible [*sic*] decision – and even when the event is plainly anti-prosperous to the high-toned machinations of the prime character, the potent, pervading hero of the story, it leaves us full of generous emotions for him; – our hearts are paralyzed –. 'Twere pseudo-philosophy to assert that we do not feel more enwrapped by the brilliancy of his career, than by the tranquil and morbid virtues of any opposing character. Our approbation of the latter is but eleemosynary...'

The truth was that Sir Edward whom circumstances had confined very much to one spot had read more sentimental novels than agreed with him ... Though he owed many of his ideas to this sort of reading, it were unjust to say that he read nothing else, or that his language were not formed on a more general knowledge of modern literature. He read all the essays, letters tours and criticisms of the day – and with the same ill-luck which made him derive only false principles from the lessons of morality, and incentives to vice from the history of its overthrow, he gathered only hard words and involved sentences from the style of our most approved writers.   SANDITON

Poetry best left to the prosaic – on the dangers of poetry for the poetic temperament:

*H*e shewed himself so intimately acquainted with all the tenderest songs of the one poet, and all the impassioned descriptions of hopeless agony of the other; he repeated, with such tremulous feeling, the various lines which imaged a broken heart, or a mind destroyed by wretchedness ... that she ventured to hope he did not always read only poetry and to say, that she thought it was the misfortune of poetry, to be seldom safely enjoyed by those who enjoyed it completely; and that the strong feelings which alone could estimate it truly, were the very feelings which ought to taste it but sparingly.   PERSUASION

On history:
It tells me nothing that does not either vex or weary me. The quarrels of popes and kings, with wars or pestilences in every page; the men all so good for nothing, and hardly any women at all . . . and yet I often think it odd that it should be so dull, for a great deal of it must be invention.   NORTHANGER ABBEY

The writer as miniaturist:
. . . The little bit (two Inches wide) of Ivory on which I work with so fine a Brush, as produces little effect after much labour . . .

(Letter to her nephew J. Edward Austen, 16 December 1816)

Flawed characters make the best in fiction:
He & I should not in the least agree of course, in our ideas of Novels and Heroines; – pictures of perfection as you know make me sick & wicked.

(Letter to her niece Fanny Knight, 23 March 1817)

STEP
parenting 101

WITHDRAWN

dr. kevin leman

www.thomasnelson.com

Published in Nashville, Tennessee, by Thomas Nelson, Inc.

Nelson Books titles may be purchased in bulk for educational, business, fund-raising, or sales promotional use. For information, please e-mail SpecialMarkets@ThomasNelson.com.

Scripture quotations are from THE NEW KING JAMES VERSION. Copyright © 1979, 1980, 1982, Thomas Nelson, Inc.

Compiled from previously published *Living in a Stepfamily Without Getting Stepped On.*

Library of Congress Cataloging-in-Publication Data

Leman, Kevin.
    Stepparenting 101 / Kevin Leman.
        p. cm.
    Includes bibliographical references.
    ISBN-13: 978-0-7852-8845-9 (hardcover)
    ISBN-10: 0-7852-8845-7 (hardcover)
    1. Stepfamilies. 2. Birth order—Psychological aspects. 3. Parenting. I. Title. II. Title: Stepparenting one hundred one. III. Title: Stepparenting one hundred and one.
HQ759.92.L46 2006
646.7'8—dc22

                                                                                    2006036056

Printed in the United States of America
06 07 08 09 WOR 6 5 4 3 2 1

Contents

What It Means to Be "Blended"

Under the best of conditions, blending a family is no snap. Chances are, you already know this is true because you are in a stepfamily situation. With a few years (or even a few months) in a stepfamily under your belt, it's very likely that the assumptions and expectations you had before your remarriage have been tempered by stark reality. A woman who remarried and wound up with five children instead of her original two told me, "We went through months of premarital counseling, but it didn't prepare us for being a blended family. Until you live with someone everyday, you and your children with him and his children, all together under the same roof, you don't know what you're going to cope with."

This woman's honest admission can be summed up in the following equation that my colleague, Dr. Jay Passavant, and I have often quoted:

E – R = D
(Expectations minus reality equals disillusionment)

Yet, despite the odds against them, despite the bruising and shattering experience of divorce (sometimes more than one), people remain intrepid eternal optimists who try marriage again. In America, the blended family has become the most common form of family in the twenty-first century. Most of the men and women who decide to remarry naively expect that *this* time their marriage and family life will work because they won't make the same mistakes. This time they have found Mr. Right or Mrs. Wonderful, and they will live harmoniously blended ever after.

Unfortunately, experience usually proves them wrong. As I try to help blended families make it, I can think of another equation that applies:

N x R = C
(Naivete times reality equals chaos)

The key to both equations is *reality*. One of the major reasons that expectations get dashed on the rocks of reality is "the kids." As one woman who married a father of two said, "The situation is just impossible. People go into these marriages with no idea of what is involved, and it's like falling off a cliff. There's never enough money to go around . . ."[1]

And she could have easily added that there is never enough time, energy, or patience to go around either. The plight of many stepfamilies reminds me of an old joke:

Question: *What's green and goes 100 m.p.h.?*
Answer: *A frog in a blender.*

A growing army of moms, dads, and children might wryly agree that another punch line could be "A blended family." And they ought to know. Stepfamily members often feel as if they're in a blender, turning green from getting whirled violently around and around—while they're being chopped to pieces in the process.

These days, with the divorce rate hovering above 50 percent, the odds are against *any* family. Put a divorced mom and her kids in the same house with a divorced dad and his kids, and those odds get even higher.

For more than twenty years, I have been working with families in my office, in seminars and other classroom settings, and on radio and television. Many of these families have involved remarriages—stepmothers, stepfathers, and stepchildren. From what I have seen, I have to admit that I often ask clients who are contemplating remarriage, "Are you absolutely *sure?* When you live in a stepfamily," I tell them, "you can get stepped on."

After all, blended families must face major issues including discipline (who will do it and how), anger, grief, and feelings of uprootedness, separation, and loss. A basic feeling I've often heard expressed by children is: "Why can't Mommy and Daddy, who are so big and powerful, solve their problems? Why can't we live together like we did before?"

Stepfamilies must also deal with the guilt everyone brings to the blended family often due to unfinished business that was left behind in a broken home. Moms and dads feel guilty because the first marriage failed, and children often believe, *If only I had behaved better—Mommy and Daddy wouldn't have gotten divorced.*

But I haven't listed all the issues. Complicating blended family life are the loyalties held by children who may feel betrayed because "Dad married this new woman, but what was the matter with the wife he had before?" Add to that the mixed histories that family members bring—different traditions, different values—that must be combined into one. And let's not forget the ex-spouses, who sometimes cause the biggest problems of all!

In later chapters, I will discuss some of these important issues, but this book will be especially unique because of its focus on birth order. Starting a blended family involves a lot more than having a Mom and a Dad and all the kids move in together. You're bringing together two sets of birth orders, and birth order has a lot to do with why family members look at things so differently from one another. Call it *different personalities,* if you please, but if there is anything a blended family needs to understand, it's *who is who and why each person is the way he or she is.*

This issue could be one of the most important issues of all: when children from two different families are brought together by the marriage of their parents, all of them are plunged into the birth order blender. After years of working with families involved in remarriages, I am convinced that the couple who understands how to blend the birth orders of their children (not to mention their *own* birth orders) has a much better chance of survival and (with lots of prayer and hard work) success. When you become aware of the significance of each person's birth order, you will be able to avoid, or at least cope with more ably, the pitfalls of remarriage with children.

BLENDING IS A PROCESS

As a counselor, I sometimes say, "Giving people hope is my business." From what I've seen of blended families, there are few who can't use a little more of that valuable commodity. As I've worked and talked with hundreds of stepparents, I've discovered that *there is hope.* There is light at the end of the tunnel. I can promise that you can burrow through the tunnel if you are patient and accept this fact: *blending is a process, not something that happens overnight.*

One of the great enemies of the blended family is the fact that we live in the age of instant everything. It is natural for Mom and Dad to assume that they will have "instant success" with their new marriage and the new family it creates. Sometimes they naively assume that because they love each other so much and because they have found the "right" mate "this time," marriage is going to be so much more wonderful the second time around, and the kids will gladly come along for the ride.

The truth is, however, that the term *blended family* is a misnomer. It's much more accurate to say that a step-family is blend*ing*. It has not become completely blend*ed,* a process that may take years—or in some cases, never takes place at all.

A glance at the various dictionary definitions will tell you that to *blend* something means mingling or combining certain components so that you achieve a measure of harmony. And that's what you're trying to do in your blending family. You want to harmonize all the various personalities while doing your best to keep conflict at a minimum and avoid discriminating against one family member or another.

It's my guess you picked up this book because you're

somewhere in the blending process. Perhaps you're about to successfully blend; or maybe you've been at it only a few short weeks or months and already you've got problems. You may be in the heart of the battle, wondering why you ever thought you could pull this off. You and your spouse may be pulling further and further apart, arguing, for example, over who should discipline whose kids (considered by many experts to be the number one issue of the blended family).

Or perhaps you're growing closer to your spouse in desperation, standing back to back as you fight off the various forces that seem to be closing in on your relationship from all sides. You're wondering how you can work it out and you're willing to try anything. *Stepparenting 101* can help. If you master these basic principles and skills described in the following chapters, I guarantee you will be much better equipped to wage the battle of blending your family and come up not only a survivor but a winner.

ONE

Birth Order Blends of Husbands and Wives

As I talk with spouses from blended families, I often ask them if the pop song Frank Sinatra made famous in the early '60s is true: "Is love lovelier the second time around?" I get a lot of quizzical looks, a few wry smiles, and very few *absolutely!*'s. Instead, I'm told, "The second time around love must be wiser—and stronger."

I often liken marriage to two people trying to play the same game with different rule books. Each spouse walks into the marriage with his or her own rule book, which is based on the lifestyle and life theme each one has developed after being born into a special spot in his or her own family. Few engaged couples ever exchange rule books or talk about them, even if they go to premarital counseling. Once they say, "I do," each spouse begins operating within the marriage according to a very personal set of rules.

It doesn't take long, however, to discover that your spouse's rule book sounds like something from a foreign land. It's not a matter of deciding whose rule book is right and whose rule book is wrong. The real challenge is for each spouse to translate his or her rule book for the other so that they can achieve harmony and understanding.

This is easily said, not easily done. By the time someone marries, his or her lifestyle has been established for years. The grain of the wood is set, and there is no changing it. You can reshape the wood, sometimes substantially by modifying your behavior and learning how to correct your weaknesses while capitalizing on your strengths; but you cannot change the grain. Your basic lifestyle is there for life.

SOME COUPLES WEREN'T BORN FOR EACH OTHER

Studies have shown that certain birth orders do better than others in a marriage relationship.[1] My own experience with hundreds of couples suggests that a good general rule for a happy marriage is to find someone as opposite your birth order as possible. In general, opposites not only attract—in marriage birth orders, they are good for one another.

Only children and last borns supposedly make the best match, followed by first borns and last borns. Then come the middle children and last borns. In case you think I'm favoring last borns as the best possibilities for marriage because I'm a last born married to a firstborn, let me assure you that these findings come from research in which I took no part whatsoever.

While there are no guarantees that being a certain birth order means that you and your spouse will live happily—or miserably—ever after, there are indicators that show which combinations work best. Following is a quick run-down of six birth order combinations and why they tend to go wrong or right in a marriage.[2]

FIRSTBORN + FIRSTBORN = A POWER STRUGGLE

The marriage of two firstborn personalities might actually

be a match between an only child and a firstborn, two
only children, or two firstborns. (Since only children are
super firstborns, we're including them in this group.) The
issues in this kind of match usually focus on perfectionism and control.

Perfectionists are the ones who can spot flaws at forty
yards or beyond. Put two firstborns together, both of
whom are very likely to be perfectionistic, and there is
bound to be a power struggle—possibly a war. In addition, two firstborn personalities can wind up butting
heads because by nature they are both used to calling the
shots and leading the way.

Tips for Firstborn Couples

1. *Steer away from "improving" on things your spouse does
or says.* Because you are probably a perfectionist, doing so
may be difficult, but bite your tongue and do it anyway.
Practice tongue control whenever possible. The New
Testament compares the tongue to the bit in a horse's
mouth or the rudder in a huge ship (James 3:3–4). Either
device turns and controls everything. The tongue can literally turn your marriage in one direction or another.

2. *Stop "shouldering" your mate.* As a perfectionist,

you are prone to be a fault-finder. Criticism is second nature to you, and not only do you criticize others, but your main target is yourself. Put away your high jump bar. Quit trying to jump higher, and quit asking your mate to do so as well.

3. *To avoid control issues, have good role definitions*—a specific division of labor as to who does what in the family. You may do the shopping, but your spouse may be the one who pays the bills and balances the checking account. Try to help each other with your assigned tasks rather than compete with each other or make things difficult. For example, if one spouse controls the social calendar, the other shouldn't make commitments without checking with him or her first.

4. *Realize there are more ways to skin a cat than your way.* This tip was especially helpful to Phil and Peggy. Phil, a meticulous firstborn controller, looked on his family as if it were a business. Peggy, his only-child spouse, had grown up with few, if any challenges of her opinion or of what she did and how she did it. Each of them needed to value the other's ideas and to learn that a suggestion that wasn't his or her own could still be a good one—even the best one—for all concerned.

FIRSTBORN + MIDDLE BORN = A NEED FOR "TELL ME MORE"

If you're a firstborn married to a middle born, rejoice in realizing you've married the most monogamous of all birth orders. At the same time, be aware that middle children can also be a vexing paradox. For example, while they have grown up having to learn how to negotiate, mediate, and compromise, they are also often secretive, preferring to keep their emotions close to the vest.

From the other side, if you're a middle child married to a firstborn, your tendency is to just throw your spouse a bone once in a while without letting him know how you really feel. If you have difficulty articulating your feelings, try writing them down and sharing them in notes that you can discuss later with your spouse. Also, take time to discuss your day or your week. Resist your natural tendency to keep feelings inside and open up to your firstborn spouse as you trust him or her to listen.

Tips for Firstborns and Middles

1. *Treat your middle child spouse special.* Give small gifts, write love notes, say the things he or she needs to

hear. Any time you do things to make a middle child feel special you are scoring points, because it's a fairly good bet he or she wasn't made to feel all that special while growing up.

2. *Work at getting your middle child spouse to articulate feelings.* By nature, firstborns are impatient know-it-alls, so back off of that tendency to keep asking your middle child spouse, "What do you think?" "Tell me how you really feel," or "Tell me more." The husband of a middle child wife often has two good reasons to seek out her opinion: First, she is probably more perceptive than he is regarding people and their feelings. Second, she's comfortable in the middle, where she can be solving and mediating problems, smoothing the way for everyone.

3. *Always assure middle child spouses that their qualities and skills are useful and needed.* In a blended family, this can mean encouraging the middle child spouse to use negotiating skills, especially on those Armageddon-like evenings when stepsiblings are battling it out. Because she's a middle child, she is probably best equipped to see both sides of a conflict and call the shots correctly.

FIRSTBORN + LAST BORN =
BLISS (USUALLY)

According to one study of three thousand families done by birth order specialist Walter Toman, the odds are best for a happy marriage when a firstborn hooks up with a last born.[3] The theory at work here is that the firstborn can teach the last born little things that are probably lacking in his or her life, like being organized, having goals and plans, and that he or she has to get serious now and then. Likewise, the last born can remind the firstborn how to relax and enjoy life.

Strangely enough, the rather huge differences between the firstborn and the last born seem to balance each other much like two people of equal weight on a teeter-totter. And it helps if the firstborn can choose a last born who, while being full of life and fun, is a little more "together."

Tips for Firstborn/Last Born Couples

1. *If inclined to fault finding, the firstborn should back off on finding the last born's flaws.* At the same time, the last born should not flaunt his flaws in the firstborn's face.

2. *The last born can teach his or her firstborn mate to hang loose and give in now and then.* In social situations, for example, when someone is late and the firstborn begins to pace the floor like a Siberian tiger, the last born can point out that a few minutes aren't going to mean the end of the world. Last borns may also be able to model for their children and spouses a generous spirit in contributing—at church or to welfares and charities.

3. *Last borns should always realize that others need their share of the spotlight.* Because last borns are performers, they sometimes forget that their firstborn mates need attention and praise, too.

4. *Firstborns and last borns can take advantage of the fact that they make a great team in the game of life.* For example, the firstborn can usually size things up better and help the last born learn to grasp the big picture and realize the impact of schedules and activities that bring pressure on the family. The last born, who is normally more of a people person, can lead the way in dealing with the feelings and emotions that circulate through the family because of conflicts that keep things from working out for everyone.

5. *Last borns can always help their firstborn mates lighten up, particularly on the kids.* Last borns, as a rule, bring the gift of fun and humor to the blended family.

MIDDLE + MIDDLE = TOO MUCH MIDDLE GROUND

Ironically, two middle children can have trouble in their marriage because they do not communicate. I say *ironically* because middle children are well-known for being great negotiators and mediators, something they learned out of necessity while growing up. Somehow, though, when they marry and start building their own families, they find it easier to keep things to themselves. Either they feel it isn't worth the hassle to confront each other, or in typical middle child fashion, they discount their own opinions.

Tips for Middle Child/Middle Child Marriages

1. *Do your best to build up each other's self-esteem.* Let your spouse know that you appreciate his or her strengths and abilities.

2. *Give each other plenty of space for outside friendships.* Because middle children are usually big on friends and social acquaintances, it's a good idea to encourage each other to have these kinds of contacts. At the same time, both of you should take care to keep friends in the "same sex" category.

3. *Always try to do something special for each other.* If you're a typical middle child, your perception may well be that no one did many special things for you while growing up. Now that you're married, you can have empathy for your middle child mate and try to make up for lost time to help him or her feel special. Remember, your something special doesn't have to cost much or take a lot of time.

4. *Don't forget that nothing is more important to a middle child than respect.* Go out of your way to show each other *mutual* respect, no matter what the situation might be.

MIDDLE CHILD + BABY = A PRETTY GOOD MATCH

When you put the middle child, typically strong in negotiating and compromising, with the socially outgoing last born, you usually come up with a healthy marriage. In fact, middle children and last borns are the third best pairing, according to birth order studies.

A plus in the marriage of a middle child and a last born is that there is a high probability for good communication—the ability to share feelings and roll with the punches. That may sound contradictory to what I said earlier about middle children tending to clam up and not share emotions, but as birth order matches go, a baby would not be as threatening to a middle child as a first-born, so the odds for good communication are better.

Tips for Middle Child/Last Born Marriages

1. *If you are a middle child mate, make good use of your tendency to want to "work things out."* That should blend well with your last born spouse's willingness to "talk it through." Be careful not to be condescending, however, because last borns can smell that in a minute. People have been writing them off in a condescending way for a long time, and their antennae can detect the tiniest slight or put-down.

2. *Work at blending your social interests with your mate's desire to be on the go.* If you're like most middle

children, friends are important and you enjoy having people over for dinner and other social gatherings. If your last born mate is typical, he will always be ready for adventure, travel, seeing new places, and meeting new people. But be aware that the daily tensions (battles) of a blended family may put a crimp in getaway plans, much to your spouse's chagrin. If opportunity ever does knock for getting away, don't hesitate. At the very least, grant in fantasy that which isn't possible in reality at the moment: "Honey, I'd love to go with you to that bed and breakfast, and we will, as soon as the kids settle down a little."

3. *If you're a last born, be brave enough to admit you probably have a selfish streak and a desire to hog the spotlight.* Try to cut your middle born mate some slack and back off now and then with your demands for service or attention. Remember, most middle children grow up feeling anything but special while many last borns grow up being pampered all the time. As the last born in the marriage, anything you can do to make your middle child mate feel a little pampered for a change will go a long way, particularly if your spouse is a stepdad who is struggling with surly stepchildren.

4. *Don't have fun at your middle child spouse's expense.*
Last borns with the typical propensity for having fun
may enjoy humor of all kinds, from practical jokes to
sarcastic little digs just to get a laugh. Keep in mind,
however, that if your spouse is like most middle children, she may be battling feelings of inferiority, and it
can be all too easy to press the wrong button. So, when
you're having fun, make a point to not do it at your
mate's expense. She'll love you all the more for it.

LAST BORN + LAST BORN = CHAOS

The marriage of a last born and a last born is not considered one of the better bets for success, and there is a certain amount of irony in this fact. After all, aren't last borns
supposed to be so sociable and communicative? That's
true, but they need to bounce off the older birth orders to
keep them in line, organized, and aware that bills come
due about every thirty days.

The big problem with last born plus last born is
answering the question, "Who is running the ship?" If last
borns don't make some firm decisions about the practical

side of life, they are headed for big-time trouble. You see, babies of the family have a tendency to forget. They also have a tendency to pass the buck and blame someone else. In a marriage, no one is a handier target than your spouse. The only problem is, if your spouse is a last born, too, guess who's catching the buck and passing it right back into your face?

Tips for the Last Born/Last Born Couple

1. *Two last borns must be aware that they can be quite manipulative by nature.* The result is that they play games with one another, often selectively hearing only what they want to hear. Later, when called to account, they respond with, "Oh, I didn't understand it that way *at all* . . . I never really agreed to do *that* . . . Why didn't you *tell me* that's what you wanted? I had no idea!" Two last borns must vow to shoot straight with each other, but not *at* one another.

2. *Learn to be active listeners.* A simple technique last borns can use to cure selective hearing is *active listening*. This means you listen with more than just your ears. You look directly at your partner and try to sense your partner's feelings as well as whatever facts are being communicated.

3. *Hold each other accountable.* If you're a last born married to a last born in a blended family, you may want to try this simple plan: Sit down at least once or twice a week and ask each other some pointed questions. "How are we doing on the budget?" "Is the checkbook under control?" "Are the kids under control?" As you hold each other accountable, be sure to use active listening and avoid being defensive. That may not be easy for two last borns who chafe under the pressures of a blended family, but use the positive skills that came with your birth order: your laid-back approach to life and your ability to handle people and stay loose in a crisis.

4. *Keep that last born sense of humor and never give up.* Never, never, never!

BIRTH ORDER IS AN ARROW, NOT THE ANSWER

Now that I have given you the "best" and the "not so good" birth order combinations for a marriage, are you encouraged or discouraged? If your birth order cards are stacked against you, or if you don't fit the typical profile, what should you do? Bail out of the blender as soon as you can? No. Birth order is only an indicator that points you in certain basic directions. What you do with your birth order—and your lifestyle and life theme—determines how you will come out in a blended family, or any family, for that matter.

The point is this: whatever your birth order and that of your spouse, it's what you make of your particular birth order strengths and how you modify and deal with your weaknesses that will decide what kind of marriage you will have. That's why love must be a lot wiser—and stronger—the second time around.

TWO

Why the Marriage Must Come First

One of the major principles I try to communicate to couples who come to me is this: *respect the way your partner sees life.* It sounds simple enough, but for some reason it's not. Perhaps it's a lot harder than it looks because seeing behind your partner's eyes involves *discovering* your partner's needs and then being willing to try to *meet* them. Meeting each other's needs is difficult enough in a first marriage, but in a second or third marriage it becomes even harder. Why? Because the partners are so busy trying to cope with all the needs of the children in their newly blended family, it's too easy to overlook the most important needs of all—*their own.*

And why are the needs of the husband and wife the most important in a blended family? What about all the children who have been brought together, all of their pain, hurt, anger, guilt, and other baggage? They are important—very important—but I still maintain that your needs and your mate's are absolutely primary. That's because you can make a stable, organized, loving home for the children in your blended family *only* when you have a strong, stable marriage relationship.

Be aware; in fact, *beware:* the typical stepfamily is a mortal enemy of a second marriage. Your kids (and your spouse's) will be out to test your relationship, and in many cases, they may even try to destroy it. Those are strong words, and you may be thinking, *Leman is exaggerating—again.*

I wish I were. You may be one of the lucky ones who is living in a stepfamily without ever getting stepped on; if so, you are rare. The facts are that in the typical step-family, the new marriage stands as a reminder to all the children of the failure of two other marriages that came before. Blended family children have had to give up their biological nuclear family for something that, in their minds at least, is second best—a binuclear stepfamily. It doesn't matter that their first family was full of tension, stress, arguing, fighting, or abuse. In their minds, it was *their home,* where Mom and Dad lived with them. Even if one parent, or possibly both, did not treat the children all that well, it doesn't matter. To paraphrase the old cliché: blood is always thickest.

Many couples realize all this when they get married— at least, they tell me they do. They understand that the children will not necessarily be that pleased. They are aware, in some cases, that the children will be downright hostile. Nevertheless, the couple is sure that they can make it work, that they can achieve the ideal of a healthy blended family. But in most stepfamilies, this ideal never becomes reality. Some stepparents and stepchildren never do blend. Perhaps they reach a state of polite truce, or maybe they develop a measure of respect for each other. But there is never a bonding equal to that between the biological parent and child.

That's okay. In fact, it's a good idea to accept that bonding with your stepchild is a nice ideal but probably won't be reality. But what you must try to do with every tool and weapon at your disposal is to bond with your spouse and make your marriage as strong and impregnable as possible. Only then will you be able to withstand the testing and probing, the poking, prying, and chipping that your kids will do to see if the two of you are "for real." And if they find they can't break you down, a strange thing usually happens. They feel more secure and settle down to blend into the family as well as they can.

But, if you and your partner want to stay strong enough not to crack under the relentless pressure that the kids will apply, you have to understand each other's needs.

WHAT DOES SHE REALLY WANT? WHAT DOES HE REALLY WANT?

Baffled husbands will sometimes plead with me to give them the answer to: "What does she really want?" I tell them I'm not sure what a woman *wants*, but after listening to several thousand of them behind closed counseling doors, I have a fairly good idea of what a woman *needs*. We counselors have different ways of describing human need, and I try to keep my list short. Admittedly, my list isn't as short as that of one husband I counseled.

When I asked him, "Do you know what your wife's

greatest need is?" he looked blank for a moment and then replied, "VISA?"

As important as those little pieces of plastic are to most modern marriages, I believe that when all of the complaints, longings, and feelings are shaken down, a wife really needs three things:

Affection: "Just hold me, hug me; we can undress later."

A stable family: "Be committed to me—and my kids . . . yes, even until death do us part!"

Conversation: "Let's talk; let's be interested in and understand each other."

As for men, what I hear them saying about their needs is this:

Sexual fulfillment: "Make love with me because you want to, not because you have to. And sometimes it would be fun if you came on to me *first!*"

Companionship: "Be my best friend."

Respect: "Recognize the role I play in this family. I'm out there busting my tail for you and the kids!"

SHE NEEDS CONVERSATION /
HE NEEDS COMPANIONSHIP

When I say *conversation* is a vital female need, I mean
women want something more than merely talking
together. This "something more" is *communication*,
which, unfortunately, has become a cliché in marriage
counseling literature. Cliché or not, communication, or
the lack thereof, is still a frequent reason people give for
getting a divorce. Running a marriage without communication is like running an engine without oil. Sooner or
later, the engine self-destructs.

Maybe a better term for communication is *conversa-
tional chemistry*. Without it, the remarried couple trying
to blend a family is severely handicapped. With all those
birth orders bouncing off one another and all those
lifestyles crossing and clashing, there is just too much
emotional input that has to be processed each day. There
are too many feelings that need sorting out, too many
opinions that need to be acknowledged and accepted,
too many misunderstandings and misconceptions that
need to be set right.

Again, a key factor that must be considered here is

time. It takes time to converse and to learn how your wife really feels. Men are notorious for being willing to settle for the facts and being seldom tuned into feelings. In the blended family, especially, emotions are running high and the wife has a lot of them. If you don't think so, just ask any stepmother who has had "another one of those days" with stepchildren who have given her gas emotionally and would like to do so literally if they had the chance!

A crucial male need that correlates somewhat with the woman's need for conversation is companionship. In *His Needs, Her Needs*, Willard Harley talks about men needing "recreational compatibility."[1] This doesn't mean that a wife has to fish, hunt, or rock climb. Ideally, it's best if you can find an activity that both of you like. Harley lists over one hundred activities that husbands and wives can consider to find things they like to do together.[2]

SHE NEEDS STABILITY/ HE NEEDS RESPECT

By now it's possible that an obvious question may have occurred to you: "Are the needs for a person in a first marriage the same as they are for a person in a second or third marriage?" For the most part, there is no difference, *except* the woman's need for a stable family. In a blended family, for many women this basic need suddenly leaps right to the top of the list. Many women who remarry are looking for a commitment to family that just wasn't there the first time around.

I have talked to many wives who got remarried to a certain man because "he looked like he'd be a good father to my children." While it is true that the marriage comes first, any man in a blended family should realize that showing love and affection for his wife and showing love and affection for her children (his stepchildren) are practically one and the same.

I will even go as far as to say that the wife in a blended family will love her husband to the degree that she knows her kids are okay. In fact, as a husband focuses on making sure his wife feels safe about having her kids around him, the way is then open to meeting her needs for affection and conversation.

Also, stepfathers must realize that parenting takes time—a *lot* of time. Most women already know this, but men tend to be more vocation oriented. They are, therefore, sometimes oblivious to the fact and need to be reminded. Willard Harley recommends that men and women try to spend fifteen hours a week together in doing mutually enjoyable recreational activities, and he adds to that *another* fifteen hours a week as a goal for quality family time where everyone is involved.[3] Does this sound too idealistic? Maybe, but it is a target worth shooting at if you want to make your blended family work.

While the most keenly felt need for husbands, bar none, is sex, a close second is respect. Men never want to admit it, but preserving their delicate male egos is very important.

This is especially true in a blended family. I've talked with many a stepfather who was baffled by his stepchildren's hostility or by their total lack of respect for anything he had to say. And quite often his wife is siding with her children, sometimes inadvertently, perhaps; but nonetheless, she is leaving her husband feeling as if he's out in the cold, shut off from the very people he is trying to blend with.

If the wife wants to score points with her blended family partner, she should seriously consider the fact that men have fragile self-images. The legendary delicate male ego is all too real. Men often look supremely confident, as if they have it together, but inside they may be coming apart. Many normally perceptive wives don't seem to grasp this. I've seen it again and again in my office: the wife criticizes the husband or complains about him. If I suggest that encouraging him might get better results, she looks at me incredulously.

On the other hand, if a husband wants his wife to show him respect, along with admiration and encouragement, he needs to demonstrate the characteristics and qualities that will motivate her to do so. As he meets her needs and gives her the feelings of security that she desperately seeks, she can't help but show him the respect and admiration he so desperately seeks in return.

One of the most encouraging examples of how this works was Ruth, who had divorced her first husband after five years of listening to his verbal abuse and grieving over his total neglect of their two boys, Ben and Casey. Her second husband, Howard, had not been married before. A firstborn, he had grown up in a very large family and had been responsible for several younger siblings. When he met Ruth, he had instant rapport with her two young sons, who responded to his affectionate hugs and "wrestling matches" with enthusiasm.

"I loved Howard's affectionate ways," Ruth said. "And he loved that I was such a good mom. So we were a great pair from the start."

When I asked Ruth what her greatest challenge was in blending her family, she said, "Trying to accept all the attention and the love and the kindness from Howard. That was the hardest part for Ben and Casey and me— just accepting all that attention, because we just weren't used to it."

GO AHEAD, TRY THIS AT HOME

Are you giving out large doses of love, attention, and respect? Spend time strengthening the most important element of your blended family—your marriage. Whatever you do, have time to focus on each other, not the kids. You will get to the kids in due time, so will I— coming up in the next chapter.

THREE

Firstborns

Whenever I conduct a birth order seminar, I can almost guarantee I'll get a question like this: "We have a blended family and now my firstborn son is really a middle child because my husband has a boy who is older than my son and a daughter who is younger. So what is he—a firstborn or a middle child?"

What this person is really asking is, "If you wind up in a different birth order position in a blended family, does that mean you become that birth order?"

My answer is maybe yes, probably no. It depends on the *timing*.

If your family blends when the children are very young, well below the age of five or six, then the answer is yes. Someone who might have been born first in his original family could grow up more like a middle child, or even a baby, if that's where the new blending places him. On the other hand, if that child is born first and his mother divorces when he's seven or eight, no matter what birth order position he takes in his blended family, he will always have a firstborn personality.

By the time a child is five or six years old, the grain of the wood is set. And the point to remember is this: *When a child who is born into one birth order lands in another position in his blended family, do not treat the child as something he is not. He may have to take on different responsibilities or play different roles at times, but never forget who he really is.* This point is so important that I am spending the next three chapters going over the typical characteristics of each birth order to show you why children (and parents) behave as they do and why blending different birth orders can be so difficult. Remember, unless children are very young, birth orders don't change, they collide.

CAUTION! BIRTH ORDER
VARIABLES AT WORK

When people hear me speak on birth order, they often marvel at how I seem to be able to describe everyone in their family "perfectly." What they don't realize, however, is that birth order is seldom as simple as "one, two, three, and everybody fits in their little slot." Being born first, second, or last (or thirteenth) sets you up with some general tendencies and characteristics, but it doesn't guarantee that you're going to come out of some kind of birth order cookie cutter.

What really matters are the dynamic relationships between you and the other members of your family. These relationships can be affected in any number of ways— what I call *birth order variables*. Actually these variables are what make birth order theory really fascinating because they explain in great part why some people don't seem to fit the "mold" of their birth order.

Occasionally someone will tell me, "I'm a firstborn, and I'm not like what you described at all. I'm messy, never in control, and always disorganized." Or someone else might say, "I'm a last born, but I'm the one who's conscientious and perfectionistic. How do you explain that?"

In every crowd there are always examples of birth order inconsistencies, and I can almost always explain these with birth order variables, such as: the order in which boys and girls arrive in the family, the number of years between the children, physical differences, the birth order of the parents (which will affect their parenting style), or the blending of families because of death or divorce.

For example, suppose a boy is born first, followed by a girl, and then another girl. Will they exhibit typical firstborn, middle child, and last born characteristics? In many respects they will, but you also have a firstborn male and a *firstborn female*, and she might come out with many firstborn characteristics of her own. Or consider a family that consists of a boy, another boy, a girl, and another boy, all two years apart. Who do you think would get the most attention in the family? The baby princess, of course. And with two older brothers, little last born prince might get the short shrift of attention.

So as you keep in mind that there are several birth order variables that can affect every child, what are the typical characteristics you can expect in birth order? Let's begin with the firstborns and only children and why they typically clash in an intimate setting such as a blended family.

FIRSTBORNS HIT THE GROUND RUNNING

With his parents as his only role models, the firstborn is constantly trying to emulate the all-powerful and all-knowing "giants" who seem to be able to do everything well and nothing wrong. Because they are so busy trying to imitate their much more capable parents, firstborns quite naturally tend to become careful planners who are detail oriented and well organized. They also tend to be serious loyal, conscientious types who "can always be counted on." Firstborns often do well in school, developing self-reliance that makes them natural leaders.

While firstborns receive more discipline than any other birth order, they get the long end of the stick in some positive ways too. One of the perks of being first-born is that anything you do is a big deal as far as Mom and Dad are concerned. Everyone tends to take firstborns very seriously, and firstborns try to live up to their confident, responsible image. Consequently many firstborns are hard-driving achievers, but many others are compliant and eager to please in addition to being achievement oriented.

LONELY ONLIES GET A BAD RAP

This is a good time to comment that the only child, first cousin to a firstborn, has all of the same characteristics—*in spades*. To put it another way, an only child is a *super* firstborn—super-perfectionistic, super-achieving, super-conscientious, and super-organized, to name a few of the firstborn traits that only children take to new frontiers.

Because only children don't have the problem of learning to share with siblings, a lot of people think they are selfish hedonists or self-centered narcissists. But according to a family therapist from Brigham Young University, research shows that only borns have great initiative, enjoy high self-esteem, and don't call themselves lonely.[1]

One of the keys to understanding the only child is to ask *why* she is the only one. If she is a special jewel because her parents wanted other children and couldn't have anymore, then she might wind up with the feeling that she's the center of the universe. But if she's an only child because her parents planned it that way, her cool, confident exterior may be covering up a frightened, rebellious, angry person who is hard on herself and her peers.

My own research and study of firstborns and only children show that either position has its perks, but it also has at least one big problem—pressure. Firstborns and onlies are under the gun from day one, continually admonished to sit up straight, shape up, do it now, take charge, and be an example.

PERFECTIONISM—DEADLY ENEMY OF THE STEPFAMILY

While perfectionists can be found in other birth orders (particularly middle children), perfectionism is the dominating burden of almost all firstborns and only children. Perfectionism haunts them like the headless horseman haunted Sleepy Hollow.

"I know I could have done better" is a telltale sign of the firstborn or only child who is carrying what I call "the albatross of perfectionism" around his neck. And when confronted with his endless, wearying quest for perfection, he often responds, "Well, if I'm not supposed to try for perfection, what am I supposed to do? Do worse than my best and just live a mediocre life?"

I always answer, "Not at all. Instead, learn the difference between pursuing perfectionism and seeking excellence." The following statements will help you learn the difference between perfectionism and excellence.

Perfectionism:
I aim for the top.
I tell myself "I should" or "I must."
I am motivated by a deep fear of failure.
I focus on the product—results are what count.
Life is a daily battle.

Excellence:
I strive to do my best.
I tell myself "I want" or "I would like."
I am motivated by the desire for success.

> *I enjoy the process involved in what I make or manage*
> *or the service I do.*
> *Life is a daily challenge.*

If you are in a blended family, make seeking excellence your goal, and keep in mind that you are modeling this lifestyle for your children who may also have a bent toward perfectionism. Forget about perfection because it simply isn't within reach. In a stepfamily, perfectionism will set you up for self-doubt and misery because you will think you are valued for what you do rather than for who you are. If you seek perfectionism in your stepfamily, the failures and disappointments that are bound to come will defeat and depress you. But if you settle for seeking excellence, you can accept disappointment and keep going. Remember, failure devastates the perfectionist, but failure is a teacher and a real help to the seeker of excellence.

Rare is the stepfamily in which a stepparent isn't criticized. If you're seeking perfectionism, you will hate the criticism (and probably the critics). If you're seeking excellence, you're more apt to welcome criticism. You may not enjoy it, but you can accept it and learn from it.

TIPS FOR FIRSTBORN OR
ONLY CHILD PERFECTIONISTS

Some general advise that I give to most stepparents include two basic principles that pertain to stepparenting no matter what birth order you might be or what kind of personality you have. First, when your stepchildren rebuff you, remember that you're in this for the long haul. Don't expect instant results, and, above all, remember that your stepchildren are the children and you are the adult. Second, as a stepparent, determine that you are going to love your spouse's kids, no matter what.

No matter what your birth order—firstborn, only child, or something else, it's possible that you are a perfectionist stepparent, and that being true, it's likely you are experiencing friction with your stepchildren. Here are a few dos and don'ts to keep in mind:

Don't be so picky with your spouse, your stepkids, your own kids, and yourself.

Don't ask so many questions, especially ones beginning with the word why.

Don't try to do it all. Learn to say no and learn to delegate.

Do be willing to laugh at your mistakes.
Do lighten up and lower your expectations.
Do try to be more positive.

As a perfectionist, you may think it's perfectly normal to alphabetize the spice rack, cover the furniture with sheets except on Christmas and Easter, and color coordinate everyone and everything in sight, but the people you live with probably don't. Your tendency to pick flaws and criticize can unblend a family faster than almost anything else. Strive for excellence, and you'll be well on your way to helping your family blend successfully.

FOUR

Middles

A major problem anyone faces in defining a "typical" middle born is that he can be in any number of positions in the family: second of three, third of four, fourth of five, and so on. As I said in my earlier work *The Birth Order Book*, the *branching-off effect* is a critical factor when dealing with a middle child. By *branching off* I mean that as each child is born into the family, he usually plays off the child just older and develops a different approach to operating in life, a different "specialty" that is personal and individual.

For example, if a firstborn is the family bookworm or

scholar, the second born might well be the family athlete or musician. Naturally some genetically inherited skills are necessary for such pursuits, but as a rule each child wants to carve out his own niche and therefore branches off in a somewhat different direction than the sibling just older.

This branching-off effect is the reason it is so hard to develop a definite and consistent list of characteristics for middle children. As you will quickly see, the following descriptions seem to cancel each other out, but all of these characteristics are possibilities for middle children because so much depends on how they bounce off their older brothers or sisters.

- Sociable, friendly, outgoing
- Takes life in stride, easy going, not competitive
- Peacemaker, mediator, excellent negotiator
- Impatient, easily frustrated
- Quiet, shy
- Rebel, family goat
- Avoids conflict

R-E-S-P-E-C-T

What can we say then is typical of the middle child? Actually there are several things, and one of the most common is this: middle children just don't feel they get a whole lot of respect or notice. The key reason that they feel so disrespected is that they feel squeezed between older and younger siblings.

Middle children will usually tell you that they didn't feel all that special while growing up. The firstborn had his spot—carrier of the family banner and responsible for everything. The last born had his comfy little role, but the middle born had no distinctive place to call his own.

Another thing that can be said of many middle born children is that they typically place great importance on their peer group. The middle child is well-known for going outside the home to make friends faster than anybody else in the family. When a child feels like a fifth wheel at home, friends become very important; as a result, many middle children (but not all, of course) tend to be the social lions of the family. While firstborns, typically, have fewer friends, middle children often have many.

Middle children have a propensity to leave home first and live farther from the family than anyone else. I observed a dramatic illustration of this tendency while I was a guest on Oprah Winfrey's show. The subject that day was sibling rivalry. Three charming young women, all sisters, were among the guests, and we quickly learned that the firstborn and the last born were residents of the Eastern state where they had grown up. They had settled down near their parents and other family members. But the middle child had moved to the West Coast. She wasn't on the outs with anyone in the family; she simply wanted to do her own thing, make her own friends, and live her own life.

MIDDLES ARE OFTEN GOOD TEAM PLAYERS

Because he feels like an outsider in his own family, the middle child often becomes a free spirit in many ways. He may be the one to reject the family values and accept his peer group's values instead. He may find his sense of connection by being part of a team (middle children are known as good team players), a club, or a gang. Whatever the group might be, the middle child sees that group as his—a second family, so to speak. No wonder he spends so much time with them. His family can't squeeze him or neglect him when he is with his other "family" on another turf.

All of this is to say that middle children do not totally ignore their siblings or the rest of the family. One common characteristic of the middle child is that she is a good mediator or negotiator. She comes naturally to this role because she's often right in the middle, between big brother and little sister, whatever the case may be. And because she can't have Mom and Dad all to herself, she learns the fine art of compromise. Obviously these skills are assets in adult life.

So, while middle children are harder to define, they do have some identifying characteristics. And, like other birth orders, the middle child may give you clues to his identity with typical expressions that he uses on a day-to-day basis: "Nobody pays attention to me" or "Could I go first for a change?"

At the same time, as he develops his negotiating and mediating skills, the middle child also says: "Let's try to work it out," "What do you think?" or "It's no big deal."

Squeezed, ignored, shown little respect, an outsider who barely makes it into the family photo album—all this makes it sound as if the middle child is doomed to unhappiness, but not so. The middle child learns to be tough and resilient and becomes on average the most well-adjusted adult among all birth orders. Hence, middle children bring valuable skills and qualities to the blended family, especially the ability to negotiate and mediate.

WHY MIDDLE CHILDREN MAKE GOOD STEPPARENTS

If you're a typical middle child, your skills in negotiating and compromising should give you an edge in building your blended family. Keep the following tips in mind:

1. *Remember how it feels to get unfair treatment.* You probably know quite a bit about getting left out, ignored, or given little or no respect. Be aware that your stepchildren have probably been feeling the same way, regardless of their particular birth order. Do all you

can to include your stepchildren, pay attention to them, and show them respect, even though they probably won't do the same for you.

2. *Remember how it feels to be easily embarrassed.* You may still be prone to embarrassment, even if you don't admit it. From your leadership position as an adult, do all you can to keep from embarrassing others in the family, particularly your stepchildren. If something embarrassing happens to a stepchild, move in with as much empathy and T.L.C. as you will be allowed to give.

3. *Avoid playing comparison games.* Avoid them like the plague. All your life you have known what it feels like to be compared to older and younger siblings in any number of areas. Be especially careful not to compare your children to your spouse's children. Accept everyone where he or she is at the moment in this blender called a stepfamily and work from there.

4. *If you're a "free spirit" middle child, don't despair.* Your blended family may be fencing you in, but duty comes ahead of desire. At least you can empathize with family members who like to do their own thing, too! On many days, that category seems to include all the kids,

your and his. Stepparents can't always indulge themselves in doing their own thing as much as they would like. When you feel an independent streak coming on, remind yourself of the First Rule of the Family, which bears repeating often: *no one person is more important than the whole group.*

MIDDLE CHILDREN MAKE GOOD ALLIES

If you're a stepparent wondering whom to enlist as an ally among the group, you might look to the middle child. At the same time, keep in mind that the middle born children in your blended family are the most secretive and most prone to embarrassment. Play your cards right with the middle child, don't come on too strong or too fast, and you may wind up with a very good friend and comrade in creating a well-blended family.

FIVE

Last Borns

At the bottom of the birth order ladder is the last born, also affectionately known as "the baby of the family." When two families blend and two last borns come together, there are usually sparks in a constant battle to be in the limelight.

When we generalize about firstborns and onlies, we usually call them serious; but when we generalize about last borns, we come up with phrases like "charming little manipulators," "precocious," or "engaging show-offs." You'll also find that last borns can be rebellious, critical, temperamental, spoiled, impatient, and impetuous. I was all of those at different times, too, as I suffered the fate of all babies who are considered the smallest, weakest, and least experienced. Naturally, last borns are not taken very seriously because they're "not big enough to do anything," or at least not anything right. In short, babies have to live in "the shadow of those who were born before," as their older siblings tend to write them off more often than not.[1]

Remember what I said about everything a firstborn does being a "big deal"? For last borns, it's just the opposite. Their first steps, their first successful tying of shoelaces, their first *anything* is more likely to be met with polite yawns or comments like, "Oh, will you look at that! Little Fred has learned to do a somersault. Remember when Timothy did that?" Without realizing it, these parents have sent little Fred a discouraging message: "Your older brother has already done what you think is so special."

As a last born, I got enough of those messages myself to develop my own rebellious streak. Mixed in with my last born charm and precociousness was the vow, "I'll show them!" That's part of the reason I was willing to risk life and limb to goad my older brother into a murderous rage at times. I not only wanted to show him up; I wanted to show him I was someone to be reckoned with.

Besides "I'll show them," there are many other typical last born phrases, many of which I uttered while growing up: "I did it just for laughs," "Won't you help me?" "I was just kidding," or "That's not fair!" Last borns may often come across as absentminded flakes who walk around with their fly unzipped or some crucial, obvious buttons unbuttoned. But they aren't as helpless and incompetent as their older siblings may think. Babies of the family are often perceptive people persons who go into professions like counseling, teaching, and sales.

HELPFUL QUESTIONS FOR LAST BORN STEPPARENTS

If you are the baby of your family and today are a parent yourself—and a stepparent to boot—here are some questions to consider:

1. *Are you a good role model?* Before demanding that your spouse and stepchildren act more responsibly, check how well you are doing as a responsible adult. Babies of the family are notorious for their irresponsibility, and maybe you are acting irresponsibly and not even realizing it.

2. *Are you messy or are you a neat freak?* Many last borns are messies. If you fall anywhere in that category, be slow to demand neatness from your stepkids when you won't be neat yourself.

3. *Are you self-centered or others-centered?* Because they're often spoiled, last borns are typically self-centered. As an adult, you have probably learned to cover up your self-centeredness quite well, but the pressures of being a stepparent may bring it to the surface. As a baby of the family myself, I know whereof I speak; it's easy for a last born to throw self-pity parties. When you feel one coming on, remind yourself of Dr. Leman's First Rule of the Family: *no one person is more important than the entire group.*

4. *How likely are you to blame others for your mistakes?* Refusing to accept blame is another classic last born trait, and if you're doing this in a stepfamily, you can get stepped on—and fast! If nothing else, you'll be stepping on others and causing bruised feelings where there are already many emotional wounds.

5. *Are you used to the limelight?* Are you the funny, gifted, charming one? If the rest of your family could be honest, what would they say about your interest

in them? Do you ask them about their ideas, their schedules, and what they think, or are you usually talking more about yourself and your plans?

6. *Do you use your gifts and skills positively?* If you're a typical last born, you have abilities that can be of great use in a blended family. For example, you may be gifted in sizing up relationships and lightening up tense situations with a little laid-back humor. You probably feel comfortable in social situations, and you like to solve problems with the aid of others. And you're also good at getting others to do things you'd like to have accomplished. Last borns are skilled at management from the bottom, meaning that you are able to persuade (and even manipulate a little bit) your way through situations that might stop others in their tracks.

DON'T LET THE LAST BORN SLIP THROUGH THE CRACKS

As last borns grow up in their natural nuclear family, they are influenced deeply by their older siblings for good and sometimes for not so good. By the time a last born is five or six, the grain of his wood is set (just as it is with any birth order). The typical last born needs, craves, and demands attention, and she gets it one way or another, sometimes by being cute and precocious, sometimes by being a little pest, or even sometimes by being a spoiled brat.

In chapter six, we'll be looking at specific techniques for parenting last borns in a blended family. For now, however, keep one thing in mind: when death or divorce smashes his little world into smithereens, the last born can be a bundle of shattered nerves or an "I'll show them" time bomb ready to explode. Blended families need to make sure that last borns don't slip through the cracks, especially if a last born from one side of the family is suddenly shouldered out of the limelight by someone younger and cuter from the other side.

As you look around your blended family, you may see someone slipping through the cracks. It could easily be a baby, or it could be someone else. It could be your natural child or your stepchild. Whoever it is, take notice of them, do something special with them, encourage them. In the end, it will be worth all the effort.

SIX

Blended Family Discipline

According to many stepfamily specialists, discipline of the children is the number one issue in the blended family. I agree. As I emphasized earlier, you and your spouse will stand or fall, sink or swim, *together,* and if there is anything the two of you need to work through to agree upon it's, "Who will discipline the kids and how will it be done?"

As you work out a system that you both can be comfortable with, a good rule of thumb for blended families is: *start out with each parent disciplining his or her own children.*

In the majority of cases I've seen, natural mothers need this rule more than natural fathers do. The natural mom is reluctant to let the stepfather discipline her

kids. If she has been living for some time as a single
mom, it's not unusual for her to have slipped into a permissive approach, and she may be reluctant to do much
disciplining, period. In other cases, however, the natural
dad may be the one who is lax, and he will tend to leave
the disciplining to his new wife, a practice that often
places her in the role of the wicked stepmother.

So to begin with, in the blended family it is best if natural parents handle the disciplining of their own children.
This should be a short-term solution, however, and in the
long-run, you want to find a system where both of you
can discipline all the children consistently and lovingly.

Stepparents should work into disciplining their
stepchildren a little bit at a time. Don't leave all the disciplining to the natural parent because this will undermine
the stepparent's position of authority in the home. I have
talked to many stepfathers who feel emasculated because
they "don't dare say anything" to stepchildren. But at the
same time, their wives are reluctant to let them do any disciplining because they think they will go too far.

Work as partners. When you do, you'll discover what
valuable allies you are for one another. One can make up
for where the other may be lacking, and vice versa.

Together, the parents form a powerful team that their children may test and even defy at times, but in the long run they will feel more secure because they finally understand that this marriage will last.

THE SEVEN SECRETS
OF LOVING DISCIPLINE

Blended family parents need a system that can help bridge the gaps between stepparent and stepchild, and reinforce love. They don't necessarily need to institute law and order, but they do need to use "love and order." Maintaining this delicate balance in a blended family is vital because you are dealing with children who have been deeply hurt by divorce (or the death of a parent). They need compassionate guidance and training plus the limits that make them feel secure and stable. Principles of discipline that I have taught consistently are described in a book I've written, *Making Children Mind Without Losing Yours.*[1] For blended families, I call this system *Loving Discipline* because it gives you a consistent, decisive, respectful approach to disciplining your children and assuring them of your love at the same time. All parents need to walk the line between authoritarianism and permissiveness, but blended family parents need to walk it with special care as they practice the following principles:

1. *Relationships come before rules.* All of the secrets of Loving Discipline must be used *gently* but firmly in order to obtain the best results. If parents in a stepfamily try to use Loving Discipline without extra sensitivity to the anger their children feel (usually because of the divorce that made their blended family possible), its effectiveness will be greatly reduced (more on anger in the next chapter).

2. *The whole is more important than the parts.* With all those birth orders bumping and crisscrossing, certain family members may try to control the entire family. When Loving Discipline is practiced consistently, all family members are treated fairly; all get equal time and equal opportunity to participate and contribute.

3. *You are in healthy authority over your kids.* In other words, you are not too authoritarian or too permissive. You strike a middle ground that some parenting specialists call authoritative. In the blended family,

the crucial question is, "How much healthy authority can the stepparent exert with his or her stepchildren?"

4. *Hold children accountable for their actions.* Loving Discipline does not *punish* but lets the child pay a reasonable consequence for misbehavior or a poor attitude. In a blended family, goals and rules must be carefully spelled out. Clearly communicate as well *who* holds who accountable.

5. *Let reality be the teacher.* Using reasonable consequences as a tool and not a weapon in the blended family is an art. When telling a blended family child, "I'm sorry, you broke the rule and now you can't go to your Little League game," you must be sure to temper firmness with friendly good humor.

6. *Use action, not words.* Make clear the kind of behavior you expect from your children, but keep the consequences varied, depending on the kind of training you believe they need in the moment. This keeps them a bit off balance, but it helps them concentrate on being responsible and accountable instead of simply trying to avoid certain predictable consequences.

7. *Stick to your guns.* This is an all-important principle, particularly when a child is wailing, crying, carrying-

on, or telling a stepparent, "You're not my father!" In a blended family especially, sticking to one's guns does not mean mowing everyone down. It means being firm in enforcing whatever rules you all have agreed upon, even when your heart is breaking for the child who has just chosen to lose an entire weekend of wonderful activities by not being responsible.

USE DIFFERENT APPROACHES TO DIFFERENT BIRTH ORDERS

Some good general rules for using Loving Discipline are: *be fair, be consistent,* and *treat each child differently.* One reason not to treat all your children the same is that each birth order responds to discipline in a different way.

Firstborns

When dealing with a firstborn of any age, be sure everyone knows the rules. Firstborns want to know exactly what is required of them, what is right and *fair.* Taking a little time to spell things out for your firstborn will pay off in many ways. This will show him that you respect him and care about him. At the same time, it gives you a better lever for using Loving Discipline.

When a firstborn does break the rules, sit down with him and ask, "Okay, what were the rules on this one?"

After he tells you, then ask, "What should be your consequence?"

Let the firstborn come up with some solutions. Before administering the obvious discipline, wait him out and see if he can come up with an idea himself. If he fails to show much imagination, then offer a logical consequence to his breaking the rules.

Disciplining the Second Born in a Two-Child Family

When disciplining children in the two-child family, remember that your second born can be a mix. He may have last born traits, but he could also have firstborn qualities, particularly if his older sibling is a different sex. When you have one of each, you really have a firstborn girl and a firstborn boy on your hands.

Sometimes treating firstborns and second borns differently may result in one of the children claiming, "That's not fair—you gave her more than me!" Acknowledge that that might be true, but next time the tables will be turned. This kind of "unfairness" evens out in the end.

Where you want to be scrupulously fair is in enforcing the rules. For example, be sure bedtimes are different for the children—even if they're only a half hour apart. Be vigilant to send the second born to bed at 8:30, while the firstborn is allowed to stay up until 9:00. If either gets to stay up later than the agreed-upon time, you will hear about it.

Make sure that responsibilities are different for the two children. Don't pile everything on the firstborn just because he proves himself to be reliable, conscientious, and willing to do it. Make a deliberate point to require the second born to hold up to his or her end. Don't be afraid to give the second born the more menial task—raking the yard, dusting the bookshelves, or sweeping the garage— even though you know the firstborn would do a better job.

Bite your tongue if you feel like saying, "Why aren't you like your brother [sister, stepbrother, or stepsister]?" The last thing your children or your stepchildren need is comparisons. Believe me, they are making comparisons at a mile-a-minute rate anyway. When a parent or a step-parent comes along and starts comparing, it only makes the pain of comparison deeper, and discipline is all the harder to administer. Always remember the cardinal rule of Loving Discipline: relationships come before rules. The reason for that is simple:

Rules without relationships lead to rebellion.[2]

Middles and Last Borns

The best approach to disciplining most middle children is to ask them, "Why?" but not with the tone of voice that puts them in a corner. Instead, give them a chance to explain themselves while you listen and don't interrupt. You could say, "I'm interested in why—what was your thinking on this? I asked you to stay with your little sister, but you came home without her and let her walk home later by herself. That's not like you. What happened?"

Asking a middle child "Why?" in this fashion tells her that you want to hear her out. Also, ask the middle child to list the pluses and minuses of what happened. Ask her, "What have we learned from this situation?" All these things help make her mistake a teachable moment in her life.

As for those lovable babies of the family, be aware that

when they goof up, they will try to get out of it. I know
because I pulled it off for years (and sometimes I still try).
The baby will look for someone else to blame. When she
says, "It's Sister's fault," just smile and say, "Okay, Sister is
in her room. You stay right here, I'm going to get her."
Then bring big sister in and have her give her version of
what happened.

The principle here is that when you feel your last born
may be pulling your chain a little, try to go right to the
source and find out what really happened. This inquiry
may make you feel somewhat like Judge Judy, a style that
I'm not usually in favor of; but when dealing with the last
born, remember that he's usually trying to get away with
murder. You need to be firm as well as loving.

On the other side of the coin, your last born may be
saying, "I'll show them!" If you think he's acted up
because he feels discounted, overlooked, or put down, sit
him down and ask him to tell you what is really going on.
If his answer is sincere and not obviously manipulative, it
can give you a better idea of what his discipline should be.

Remember the baby is the slipperiest birth order of
them all. When he breaks the rules, be sure you follow
through with consequences. If you let him off the hook,

he will shamelessly take advantage of everyone—and charm your socks off while he does it.

WHAT MAKES LOVING DISCIPLINE SO DIFFICULT?

Now that I laid out my "perfect" system for disciplining children, you might be saying, "All this sounds great, Dr. Leman. I guess you've been able to pull it off with your kids, but when I try some of this stuff with mine, they don't come back with just the right actions. It's still hard—very hard."

I couldn't agree more. I've had some hard moments myself while raising five kids (I still do, now and then). I still believe, however, that the secrets of Loving Discipline are the best approach to raising responsible, accountable, and *affectionate* kids.

Before using Loving Discipline on your kids, however, be sure you have discipline in your own life. The best way to teach your kids responsibility and accountability is to model those characteristics yourself.

SEVEN

Blended Family Enemy Number One

Disciplining the children may be the number one issue among most blended families, but anger is the villain that is causing most of the discipline problems.

You can almost bet that *everyone* in a blended family is mad at someone or someone is mad at them. Stepmoms are mad because they are treated like dirt or like the maid. Stepdads are mad because all they seem to be good for is paying the bills. Kids are mad because one of their parents is gone, sometimes forever. Children in the blended family are especially angry because they have been "ripped." They are hurt, and often they want to hurt back.

WHAT CAUSES THE ANGER?

Many of the issues facing the blended family are deep-seated causes of anger among its members, especially the kids. When we put those issues in the form of questions, we can see why the anger is there. Here are two familiar examples:

"Why can't I see my dad more often? . . . Why can't Dad come back and live with us? . . . Why did Mommy have to die?" Questions like these pinpoint the *separation* and *loss* that the child feels after divorce or death. And now that he's in a new family, these feelings of loss affect his thoughts, decisions, and actions. Even if a child's family was dysfunctional (cold, neglectful, or abusive), it was still *his family*, and he hated to lose it. His blended family reminds him daily of what he has lost. There is no instant cure for the pain caused by this separation and loss. Each person must learn to deal with it and let time be the healer.

"Why did we have to move? . . . I liked it where we lived before . . . I miss my old friends." These comments voice the frustration a child feels from being uprooted. Moving into a blended family usually means tearing up

roots and leaving the familiar surroundings that you knew earlier. The people in your blended family have lived in three homes in the past few years: the home that was broken up due to death or divorce; the home in which they lived with a single parent; the home in which they live now in a blended family.

Everyone in a blended family has to pass through these three phases, and even if their physical location stays the same throughout, the atmosphere of these homes is much different. No one in a blended family can feel a real sense of roots, at least not right away. It will take months, sometimes years, to get rid of the uprooted feeling.

ANGER AND GRIEF GO HAND IN HAND

Working through anger caused by separation, loss, or uprootedness is a necessary part of working through the grief caused by the destruction of one of the most precious possessions in all the world—a person's original home and family. Grief includes at least three stages: shock, anger, and recovery.

Shock includes emotions like denial, numbness, and incredulity. When somebody in the shock stage says, "I can't believe it!" that's exactly what he means. He just simply can't accept what has happened. Shock can last a few minutes, or it can go on for several days or weeks. In extreme cases, it can last even longer.

For most of the people in a blended family, the shock wore off quite awhile ago. But it's a good bet that most, if not all, of them are in stage number two—*anger,* which also includes fear, depression, and apprehension. Anger is the most dangerous stage of grief because a person can get stuck there for a long time. It's common for members of a blended family to bury their pain, but sooner or later it bubbles up when they have "had enough."

Given time, anger fades and a person reaches the stage called *recovery.* She comes to terms with her pain, and while it still may be there, she can accept what happened without feeling that same slow burn and bitterness that she knew in the past. When everyone reaches at least some degree of recovery, you are not only a blended family; you are a mended family. Carolyn Johnson, a mother with four children who remarried a man with five, writes, "As we have mended our lives

and those of our children, we have also men[...]
brokenness."[1]

Brokenness may not be the most politically or social[ly]
correct term these days, but in a blended family it is a
fact that has to be dealt with. If you hope to guide your
blended family toward mending its brokenness, you
must first mend your own.

Realize, however, that mending brokenness doesn't
mean going back and assembling the broken pieces of
what once was. There is no point in kidding yourself by
entertaining the Humpty-Dumpty fantasy (besides, I have
it on good authority from stepchildren and stepparents
alike that Humpty Dumpty didn't fall; he was *pushed*). At
any rate, Humpty Dumpty can't be put together again;
you must build something new, and you do this by learning to accept the less-than-perfect situation.

CAN YOU LIVE WITH
LESS THAN PERFECT?

It's amazing how many people have trouble accepting the
less than perfect. Parents, stepparents, natural children,

nt something they can't really have.

have it, but they continue to tie

wanting it and expecting it; and

, they continue to be angry.

different, but that doesn't make

second class. As your blended family

mends its brokenness and learns to accept the less than perfect, a strange thing happens. You realize that what you had before wasn't really perfect either. In fact, *the perfect does not exist.*

All of us must find happiness and contentment in what we have. For blended families, the saying "Bloom where you are planted" is not just a prosaic platitude. It is a way of life.

Don't hurry anyone in your family who seems to be having a hard time getting over grief. Everyone grieves at his or her own pace. For some, grief comes like waves; for others, it settles like a misty rain.

Some people wonder if it's healthy to go on grieving. After all, surely it's not good to dwell upon these things. Be positive with the person whose grief and anger continue. No one can do a person's grieving for him, and no one can set a time limit on how long someone else should grieve. It's more important to be patient and loving, realizing that a child's (or a spouse's) grief may be displayed in all kinds of symptoms: weeping, nightmares, bed wetting, depression, contempt, insolence, defiance, four-letter words, and angry outbursts of all kinds.

My advice to any parent who has to handle anger that is going off in his or her face includes the following:

1. *Expect the best from everyone, but don't be surprised when anger does erupt.* Like the molten rock in a volcano, anger is bubbling and seething beneath the surface, and every now and then there is bound to be an explosion. It will not help much, however, if you explode back.

2. *Try to identify the real problem.* It may be the other person's problem completely, and realizing that will keep you from getting sucked into trading angry shots with the other person.

3. *To get at the real reason behind your stepchild's anger, listen for his or her feelings.* Earlier I touched on this briefly when talking about how to deal with your spouse, but active listening is also a valuable tool to use with children. To actively listen means that you are

trying to reflect back the feelings you are hearing your stepchild express, but as you do so you never judge, advise, lecture, or play travel agent for guilt trips.

When reflecting a child's feelings, one of the best phrases to use is "sounds like" as in, "Sounds like you are very upset with me [or your brother, or your stepdad]."

The phrase "tell us [or tell me] more" is also a very handy tool. Use it often to get the child to tell you what is on her mind. And bite your tongue when a brilliant flash of genius inspires you to lecture or give advice. I'm not saying you should never give your child advice; I am saying, try to wait for your child to ask you for it. If you feel you must offer advice, particularly to an angry child, always preface it with, "I could be wrong, but . . ."

Another effective technique that I have used for many years when dealing with an angry child during a counseling session is that when you see the child ready to tear up, just reach across and gently touch him—on the arm or on the shoulder. You don't have to say much; just let your look of compassion tell him that you want to be supportive as you listen to the feelings he's expressing.

TURN FRUSTRATION INTO
FORGIVENESS

Living in a stepfamily requires skill in handling two kinds of anger—theirs *and* yours. It's all very well to encourage family members to express feelings as you actively listen to an irate stepchild or spouse going off in your face, but just how do you deal with the rising frustration that is filling your own emotional balloon to the busting point? Here is a simple plan for keeping your cool when frustration strikes.

Frustration is stage one in moving toward an angry outburst. Simply stated, it means *not getting what you want.* If you are frustrated long enough, you are likely to begin to lose patience. Now you are moving into stage two—*indignation* (what some call "getting a little bit irritated"). You begin to think about how awful this frustrating problem is becoming. You start to tell yourself, "This isn't right . . . I don't deserve this . . . I will demand my rights!" At this point, you are entering stage three—*heated anger*, which, temporarily at least, can turn reason into insanity and love into hatred. Your emotional balloon can take no more, and you explode.

When living in a stepfamily starts to make you feel stepped on, you can head off explosive anger by using cognitive discipline. Don't follow your feelings; think it through by asking yourself, "Is this frustration a catastrophe or just an annoyance? If it really is an annoyance, must I think it is 'awful'?" Then ask yourself, "Okay, I admit I'm getting irritated, but is this the end of the world? Does this *really* matter? A hundred years from now, will it makey *any* difference? In fact, in *one year*, or even *one week*, will I even remember this?"

At this point you may be thinking, *All Leman is dgoing is giving me a fancy way to count to ten.* Maybe so, but the more you are able to cut frustration off at the ankles and not let it turn into anger, the more you will be able to cope with the times that are truly explosive. In other words, there are many situations where you can fight back by simply choosing not to fight back at all. You don't have to like what is going on, but you can accept it and hope and pray for better days ahead, which eventually do come.

And to deal a death blow to frustrations or anger, you can always whip out your most powerful weapon of all—*forgiveness.* I'm not going to preach a sermon on forgiving, but it is sort of interesting that the Bible has a great deal to say on the subject. One of my favorite passages instructs me to forgive seventy times seven (see Matthew 18:21–22). That's 490 times. I heard our pastor say once that seventy times seven is not to be taken literally. Good thing. Otherwise, a lot of parents and stepparents wouldn't take long to run out of forgiveness.

Actually, I'm told that forgiving seventy times seven really means forgiving *indefinitely*, on an *unlimited* basis. Your blended family is a perfect laboratory to experiment with this radical idea. Actually, it's more that just an experiment. Forgiveness is love in action; in fact, "Forgiveness is love's toughest work and love's biggest risk."[2] So, why not take the risk? It beats feeling stepped on every time!

EIGHT

Win/Win Blending

I believe that whenever a family is hitting on all birth order cylinders, it's because they share the same positive, healthy, wholesome values and beliefs. They have a system for operating their family that includes rules and order tempered by love, compassion—and plenty of good humor.

I was doing an all-day seminar in a small town somewhere near the middle of nowhere, southeast of Tucson. Toward the end of the afternoon, just before the final session, we took a break and a young woman who looked to be in her late twenties approached me hesitantly.

She was short and had a few too many pounds, and

while neat and clean, her clothes and hairdo were not really something out of *Vogue*. I suppose I was guilty of stereotyping again, but she had the look of someone who knew what being a mom was all about, even at her rather young age.

It turned out I was right. She introduced herself and got right to the point: "We're in a blended family. We have five kids: two of his, two of mine, and one of ours."

She mentioned that she had an eleventh-grade education, and when she and her husband had remarried, they had both attended a class to learn parenting skills at a local community college.

"I'm sure you'll be interested in the textbook we used," she said with a smile. "It was your book *Making Children Mind Without Losing Yours.* When I heard you were going to be doing this seminar, I knew I couldn't stay away. My husband wanted to come, too, but he had to work today. I got up at five o'clock this morning and drove 120 miles to get here in time. I just wanted you to know that it's been hard, but we've made it."

Always on the alert for some good input, I said, "If you'd be willing, I'd love to have you tell me what advice you'd give to somebody who's trying to blend a family."

She smiled again, and her five-foot-three-inches seemed to grow taller before my eyes as she said with authority, "Number one, you and your mate have to stand together. If you don't stand together, you don't make it."

That sounds familiar, I thought to myself.

"Second, don't push the kids . . . never force them to love each other. I've made it a point to tell my husband's children and my own that they don't have to love each other, but they do have to treat each other as well as they treat the neighbors."

That sounds awfully familiar, too, I mused. *Has this woman somehow managed to gain access to my computer?* She went on: "And another thing that we've been strong on is telling the kids they have to solve their own problems. We always insist that they work things out among themselves. We won't settle their fights for them."

This is too much, I reflected. *She not only read* Making Children Mind, *she's using it!*

"You've made my day," I chuckled. "I'm impressed with your common sense and wisdom. I've been talking to a lot of stepfamilies, but I've never heard better advice put so succinctly. You have your own Ph.D. in 'Blended Family.'"

"And you know what the funny thing is?" she added. "We've all grown to really love each other."

I could see that in her eyes. It was the same look I had seen in well-blended families before, something that made you know there was a connection—a blend of spirits. I told this mother that I was honored that she'd come all that way for my seminar. She apologized for not being able to stay for the final session—she had to get back home to get to her part-time job.

"I just wanted to say thank you for all the help you have been to our family," she said as we parted. I thanked her as well. She had been more help to me than she would ever know.

Later, as I drove into a blazing Arizona sunset, I thought about the blended family mother of five and hoped she'd made it back safely in time for work. I wondered about the home where she and her husband and children lived. Judging by the way she was dressed, they didn't have a lot of money. It was doubtful they had enough bedrooms for five kids and themselves. Perhaps they were trying to scrape money together to buy a bigger house—I didn't know.

In the eyes of many people, this family would probably

be labeled as "not having much," but in the ways that count, they actually had it all. They had rules in their family, but they understood that relationships came first. Oh, they had their struggles, arguments, and problems, I was sure, but what had she said? *It had been hard, but they had made it.* And then there were those special words, spoken with such a glowing smile: *We've all grown to really love each other.*

Those words kept coming back, reminding me of a biblical passage known to millions, which talks about faith, hope, and love, and the greatest of these being love. And wasn't there something in there about love never failing?

I thought of the many families I knew who had everything—education, position, and practically every book on parenting ever written. And yet many of these families—some natural, some blended—had failed, even though the parents had worked so hard to make sure that their children would "have everything they didn't have when they were kids."

And that's the problem. People get so busy with their schedules and agendas, living in the fax-lane of life. They have no time to spend with their children, so they try to placate them with things. But kids really don't need all those things that their parents didn't have. They need loving discipline. They need to know that somebody really cares.

The sun was going down now behind the distant mountains, and there was just a red glow left in the sky. As the last rays of daylight failed, it struck me that many things fail. Cars, appliances, and gadgets wear out. Plans, strategies, and tactics backfire; formulas and carefully designed systems don't always work perfectly—including mine! But a blended family doesn't have to fail, and it won't as long as Mom and Dad keep the goal in sight: that day when they can say, *We've all grown to really love each other.*

Notes

Introduction

1. Barbara, Hustedt Crook, "His, Hers, Theirs—Binuclear Family Ties," *Cosmopolitan,* August 1991, 76, 78.

Chapter 1

1. See Walter Toman, *Family Constellation* (New York: Springer Publishing Co., Inc., 1976). Toman studied 3,000 families before coming up with his conclusions. In a smaller study, Dr. Theodore D. Kempler, University of Wisconsin, researched 256 business executives and their wives and also discovered that certain birth order combinations made better marriages than others. The smaller study is documented in Lucille Forer's book, *The Birth Order Factor* (New York: David McKay Co., Inc., 1976), 187-88.

2. For more detailed information on birth orders, see Kevin Leman, *The Birth Order Connection* (Fleming H. Revell Co., 2nd edition, 2001).

3. Toman, *Family Constellation.*

Chapter 2

1. Willard F. Harley, *His Needs, Her Needs* (Old Tappan, NJ: Fleming H. Revell Co., 1986), chapter 6.

2. Harley, 79-80.
3. Harley, 83-84, 141-42.

Chapter 3

1. Karen Peterson, "Kids Without Siblings Get Their Due," *USA Today,* March 1, 1993, 1D.

Chapter 5

1. Mopsy Strange Kennedy, "A Last-Born Speaks Out—At Last," *Newsweek,* Nov. 7, 1977, 22.

Chapter 6

1. Kevin Leman, *Making Children Mind without Losing Yours* (Old Tappan, NJ: Fleming H. Revell Co., 1984).
2. This statement is attributed to Josh McDowell, author and widely known speaker at high school and college campuses across the United States and other countries. Josh is also the father of four children.

Chapter 7

1. Carolyn Johnson, *How to Blend a Family* (Grand Rapids: Pyranee Books, Zondervan Publishing House, 1989), 9.
2. Lewis B. Smedes, *Forgive and Forget* (New York: Pocket Books, 1984), 12.

About the Author

Internationally known psychologist, award-winning author, radio and television personality, and speaker, Dr. Kevin Leman has taught and entertained audiences worldwide with his wit and common sense psychology. He has appeared on *Oprah*, CBS's *The Early Show*, *Today*, and *The View* with Barbara Walters. Dr. Leman is a frequent contributor to CNN's *American Morning*, and he has served as a consulting family psychologist to *Good Morning America*. Some of Dr. Leman's books include *The Birth Order Book*, *Making Children Mind without Losing Yours*, *Sex Begins in the Kitchen*, *Sheet Music*, *Seven Things He'll Never Tell You . . . But You Need to Know*, and *What a Difference a Daddy Makes*. Dr. Leman and his wife, Sande, live in Tucson, Arizona and are the parents of five children.

For information regarding books, videos, and speaking engagements, please contact Dr. Leman at:

Dr. Kevin Leman
P.O. Box 35370
Tucson, Arizona 85740
(520) 797-3830 phone
(520) 797-3809 fax

www.lemanbooksandvideos.com
www.matchwise.com